Praise for Julianne Wurm's Work

"Research shows that children benefit significantly when learning environments meet well-defined measures of high-quality early care. Julianne addresses the need to do things differently and provides the tools to rethink our practices to better meet those measures. This book provides a journey for American educators to open their minds, reflect on their practices, and begin to meet children where they are."

—Michelle Cutler-Ervin
Director, Child Development Center, Central Georgia Technical College

"The reflect and connect section at the end of each chapter will play a critical role in professional growth for those who choose this path that honors and respects children and their deep ability and eagerness to question and seek. The book has a consistent message: what we believe about children is evident in the choices we make. I recommend it for those who are intrigued about Reggio-inspired practices and need permission and guidance not to be perfect, but to embark on the journey."

—Cheryl Priest, EdD
Associate Professor, Human Development and Family Studies
Faculty Director, Child Development and Learning Laboratory
Central Michigan University

"*Working in the Reggio Way* is a book I keep on my bookshelf in school as a must-read for new teachers. It is easy to use and thorough, and it gives the novice a wonderful starting point to embrace the Reggio Emilia approach. It is clear, practical, and very user friendly. A great guide for the beginner."

—Nancy Drescher
Director, Family Annex Preschool, New York City

"*Working in the Reggio Way* has been a go-to book for our Reggio study group. New members find it easy to read and the perfect introduction to the approach, while the more experienced members use it as a guide for focused self-reflection."

—Jackie Saggio
Preschool teacher and facilitator of the Cleveland Reggio study group
Communication Coordinator, Cleveland Association for the Education of Young Children

MORE

Working in the Reggio Way

Julianne P. Wurm

Cover by Brad Norr Design

ISBN: 978-0-9911658-0-3 (print)

The views expressed in this publication are those of the author, representing her own interpretation of the philosophy and practices of the Municipal Infant-Toddler Centers and Preschools of Reggio Emilia. The content of this publication has not been officially approved by the Municipality of Reggio Emilia or by Reggio Children in Italy; therefore it may not reflect the views and opinions of these organizations.

For reprint permission, email julianne@juliannewurm.com.

For more about Julianne Wurm
and to receive updates and new content,
visit www.juliannewurm.com.

Manufactured in the United States of America

18   17   16   15   14   1   2   3   4   5

To my father, James Wurm,
for always encouraging me to follow my muse.

Contents

Chapter 3

American Challenges

Chapter 4

Assemblea and the Pedagogy of Listening

Foreword

Celia Genishi

Professor Emerita, Teachers College,
Columbia University

n the pages to come, Julianne Wurm writes about working in the Reggio way in an accessible, refreshing, and invitational style—invitational above all. In her conversational voice she invites readers to learn with her, to learn what it means to make children the true center of early childhood practices. Threaded through the conversation are key definitions. Take, for example, the Italian word *protagonista*. Of course it means "protagonist," and through concrete examples Julie makes it clear that in the Reggio way the protagonist or main character is always the child. The child is trusted to be a learner and a teacher, to have interests and preferences, and to be able to share interests, preferences, and accomplishments via multiple modes of expression and communication. The child is simultaneously a family member and a community member, a player, a learner of languages, an artist, a mathematical thinker, a reader, and so on.

As Julie points out, in many cultural contexts, including the United States, adults often lack the power to position children as versatile protagonists at the center of the curriculum because academic requirements take center stage. In this book you will see illustrations of how the academic "basic" of reading might be incorporated in the Reggio way. Instead of a list of specific skills that children must master, Julie discusses how individual children may be invited to bring in and share a favorite book in the context of a daily gathering like morning meeting or, in Italy, the *assemblea*. In the current climate, where prescriptive standards are emphasized in many schools, the example of a child's experience with reading is refreshingly simple and direct. Through concrete examples like this, readers are invited to imagine classroom life where changes are possible. They unfold one small step at a time.

By placing these steps within the daily *assemblea*, Julie places teachers alongside the child, who is central but is also supported in countless ways by adults from their family, community, and classroom. In other words, although the Reggio way is "child-centered," there is never a setting in which children are flying solo. Further, practitioners can expect specifics in this book about teaching, learning, and documenting or keeping records about the heart of Reggio practices, the *intento progettuale*, or intended projects. Projects incorporate and follow children's and teachers' interests and strengths and cut a broad swath as Julie illustrates in chapter 3, when she wonders whether the intent of a project is for children to "celebrate color, complexity, or one another?" Within this rich context readers can also expect comparisons and contrasts between the Reggio interpretation of projects and that of educators in other cultures.

Some readers will already be familiar with terms like *protagonista*, *assemblea*, and *intento progettuale* because they have read Julie's first book, *Working in the Reggio Way*. These readers will discover new and thought-provoking examples of the fundamentals of working in this way, while they deepen and broaden their understanding. All readers will gain from Julie's own learning process, particularly from the thousands of practitioners who have asked her challenging questions over the years during professional development events. In short, Julie consistently and persistently invites readers to be informed, refreshed, and challenged to step up. True to the Reggio way, she challenges herself at the same time. For example, in the last chapter of the book, she describes her recent research study in a style that invites readers to step up with her—to step beyond their current locations geographically and cognitively to begin to explore the possibilities of formal research. Be assured that in the Reggio way the invitation to learn more is always open.

Acknowledgments

'd like to offer special thanks to many who have supported me and my work over the years. To begin, Beth Wallace, my editor, who helps shape my ideas and bring them to life. A heartfelt thanks to my colleagues from Reggio who taught me so much. Additionally, I will always be grateful for the opportunity afforded to me by the city of Reggio, Reggio Children, and the teachers with whom I worked. A thank-you seems inadequate to express my gratitude. It has been a blessing to be able to work with so many teachers and schools to improve the education and lives of children.

To Celia Genishi, an unwavering supporter for the better part of the last twenty years. Thanks is inadequate for all you have done.

Many other people have cheered, critiqued, collaborated, and shaped me in many ways—most importantly, the teachers, school directors, professors, graduate students, and educators of all sorts who have reach out to me, challenged me, engaged in dialogue, and pushed me to be clearer, more reflective, more articulate. They have provided opportunities for questioning and discussion that have continued to push my thinking. This book is about and for all of the educators who have worked with me, even if we have never met in person, to evolve their practice and the quality of early education. Thanks to each of you.

On a personal note, many friends and allies have listened (mostly) and told me to keep going. A sincere personal thanks to Sue and Jason Johnson, my trusted and thoughtful sounding boards and my San Francisco spare room. To Lone and Gary Foss, my family of friends and constant cheerleaders. To Dan Ariely, for the clarity you provided in many instances. To Valentina Imbeni, for the opportunity to work with Italians in America and deepen my own understanding. To Mark Alvarado and Linda Luevano, for your advice and friendship through the years. To Samantha Fair, for always being up to try something new. To Rona Frederick for our continued friendship and dialogue, since our first year teaching together in 1992. To Connie

Frances Avila, the best listener I know. All of you have helped me as a person and a thinker. Thank you.

And as always and more importantly, to the children we teach and the teachers who serve them. This book is for each of you.

Introduction

What has come to be known as the Reggio approach began after World War II, when the Italian government gave each *provinca*, or town, a small amount of money to use for a project of its choosing to help restore the sense of community. Most towns built community centers to offer a place for people to gather and socialize. In Villa Cella, a zone slightly outside the center of the small city of Reggio Emilia in northeastern Italy, the inhabitants decided on a different course: they built a school. The original concept was a *scuola del popolo* "school of the people." Loris Malaguzzi (1920–1994), a local educator who became involved in the movement to create the schools, rode his bike from the center of town to the school to see if what he had heard about was actually happening: a collection and collaboration of parents building a school for their children. When he saw what the community and parents were doing, he said, "We need to change the definition of the word 'impossible' in the dictionary." He became the school's founding director.

Malaguzzi went on to become the driving force behind the educational approach used in Via Cella and the schools in Reggio Emilia that evolved from that first *scuola del popolo*. Those schools were first brought to international attention when the Reggio approach was deemed the best in early childhood education according to *Newsweek* in "The 10 Best Schools" (December 2, 1991).

In Reggio education, teachers understand their work as taking place within a "cycle of inquiry" that they use alongside their pupils to investigate the world. Central tenets of Reggio-inspired practice include documentation of children's and teachers' work and thinking, the view of the environment as the third teacher, and understanding the child as the protagonist of the learning work.

I first learned about Reggio when I visited Italy in the summer of 1997 and was told of these famous schools. When I returned to New York and tried to do more research on exactly what made this approach unique, I could not find much information from a firsthand perspective. So I decided to move to Italy. In the summer of 1998, I went to Reggio Emilia with the hopes of working inside the preschools. First I spent a year learning Italian, and then I was granted permission to begin a full-time internship for the 1999–2000 school year. I spent my second year in Italy working at Scuola dell'infanzia Pablo Neruda. In 2000–2001, during my third year in Italy, I analyzed over one thousand pages of notes I had taken during my internship, while continuing my relationships with the students and teachers, and following projects begun in 1999.

In 2005, I released my first book for US teachers about the Reggio approach, *Working in the Reggio Way*. The response was overwhelming: both warm and authentic. I took seriously my colleagues' desire to learn; I spent a number of years traveling around North America hosting workshops and working with schools. I offered webinars and online classes during periods when the travel got to be too demanding. Through all of these wonderful opportunities I heard many of the same questions. Teachers were struggling with how to make this kind of thinking work within their cultural paradigm. They wanted permission and guidance not to be perfect, and simply to embark on the journey. Teachers' initial delight morphed into discouragement, as they measured themselves against the original Reggio schools. This comparison is like a beginning swimmer trying to compete with an Olympic athlete. It is unrealistic and completely deflating.

I found myself often in the position of cheerleader and encourager. I would say things like, "You have to start somewhere, and the same was true in Reggio. They have had fifty years of this practice." I wanted US teachers to try something new, easing out of their comfort zones even a little bit. I saw how scary it could be, how it could make teachers feel uncertain. But I wanted them to recognize that the process of changing their teaching practice even incrementally to include elements of the Reggio style of teaching and learning is both slow and time-consuming—but ultimately rewarding.

What I have come to understand is that while US education is making strides, there are still gaps between the American educational system and the Reggio approach. In this follow-up to my first book, I include more explicit information that has been culled from my travels about important aspects of Reggio, like documentation and the role of questioning. I also share some insights into the specific difficulties for American teachers in trying to work in the Reggio way: letting go of control, stepping outside the American paradigm, and making changes that are culturally appropriate for Americans. I have learned how hard it is for educators to make sweeping changes in their programs, for a number of reasons. I hope to stretch the reader's perspective of what is possible, an important step along the journey to making the seemingly impossible a reality.

My own practice has continued to evolve in the years since *Working in the Reggio Way* was published. I have spent time researching documentation more deeply, and I have looked at developing documentation practices as a way to deepen teacher practice daily inside the classroom. Documentation has been helpful in setting teachers along a path that empowers them to engage and reflect with colleagues and in communities instead of looking to one source for approval or validation. US teachers are co-constructing every day with their students and colleagues, just as teachers have been doing in Reggio for the last sixty-odd years.

This book is intended to continue as well as deepen the conversation begun in 2005 about how to use Reggio-inspired practices in an American setting. The content here is in response to the thousands of educators I have worked with who said they wanted and needed more information. I have addressed the topics that are most commonly asked about in my workshops and classes, including morning meeting, projects, and documentation. I have also included recent research I conducted as part of my doctoral work, using teacher experiences to gain a better understanding of how documentation can be useful to teachers.

How to Use This Book

If at all possible, I suggest that you work with this book as part of a group or community of practice. While the journey of professional development is always valuable, there is a lot to be said for having others to discuss and challenge your thinking. Sharp people sharpen one another. So if you can, find at least one colleague to join you on your journey. Otherwise, you can work through the book on your own.

This book builds on the content from the first book, but it's not necessary to have read or worked with the first book before starting this one.

The chapters of the book are presented in a logical order, but they also stand alone. So if morning meeting is your challenge, start with chapter 4. Use the information in whatever order is most helpful to you.

One of my goals is to help you cultivate the habit of reflection. Use a notebook to accompany the process, and document your experiments and the changes in your practice over time, as well as your questions and the ideas you want to explore further. This will serve as a reflective journal and a record of your own development as a professional. It will help you keep track of your new thinking, and you can revisit your questions as you gather more experience and knowledge.

At the end of each chapter is a section called "Reflect and Connect." When you get to this section, or any time you have a new insight or question, take a moment (or an hour, a day, or a week) to pause in your reading. Put down the book, and pick up your journal. Ask yourself how the questions relate to your practice. Expect that the book will unfold in a nonlinear fashion, as you explore in fits and starts, with lots of side journeys and looping back before moving forward. I hope you enjoy the ride.

MORE

The wider the range of possibilities we offer children, the more intense will be their motivations and the richer their experiences. We must widen the range of topics and goals, the types of situations we offer and their degree of structure, the kinds and combinations of resources and materials, and the possible interactions with things, peers, and adults.

—Loris Malaguzzi in *The Hundred Languages of Children*

Chapter 1

American Education and Reggio-Inspired Practice

Like all curricula, Reggio-inspired practice begins with a way of thinking about and viewing children. All learning and schools are situated within culture. A microculture is built into the classroom, but it also resides within a school, within a neighborhood, and within a city, and all of these are permeated by the larger culture. It's hard to see culture—it just seems like "the way things are," "the way you do it," or "common sense"—but culture informs choices and viewpoints.

This book challenges you to get even deeper inside Reggio-inspired thinking and your own practice as well, looking at ways in which they align from additional vantage points. Wooden furnishings and a light table simply are not enough to call a program "Reggio-inspired." Although the environment is vital to supporting the collaboration, theory building, and creation in the space where learning happens, what matters is what takes place within the school and how teachers think about the learning and the students. Reggio-inspired practice is about the work teachers are doing and the beliefs they have about the potential and rights of children, which translate into all of the little cumulative decisions that comprise the overall learning experience. Changing these details bit by bit can change your practice.

In my first book, *Working in the Reggio Way*, I led you through looking at your view of the child, the teaching environment, your concept of time in the classroom, the idea of *progettazione* or learning projects, observation and documentation, and the role of families in the school and children's learning.

In this book I want to challenge you to take your Reggio-inspired work with children further. The most vital step in implementing Reggio-inspired practice is to shift our approach to schooling. Many American teachers have legitimate confusion about how and where to begin Reggio-inspired practice in American schools. At the same time, they have a deep desire to better educate children. The goal of this book is to offer more ideas and opportunities for critical reflection; it's intended to accompany teachers who are moving along the path toward creating schools that are reflective of how children learn and what works for them.

Here's what we'll explore:

- the current American approach to young children's education
- Reggio ideas about how children learn
- ways to shift what you do and how you do it, starting from your own ideas about how children learn
- common challenges to Americans who want to move toward the Italian stance

- how this information came to be: my post-Reggio research on children and learning

I recently had breakfast with the father of two young girls who are four and five years old and attend a Reggio-inspired school. The father asked me what "Reggio-inspired" meant. He was worried about the quality of education his children were receiving because the school had absolutely no structure. "Is this what Reggio-inspired education is supposed to look like?" he asked, "Or is it just poorly executed in this particular setting?" He told me about his observations: running and chaos; a lack of structure, books, and instruction—in his eyes, a lack of learning. He is not the first person who has engaged me in this conversation. I have seen with my own eyes in many schools a sort of throw-your-hands-in-the-air kind of freedom that can be couched as "following the children's interests." This kind of execution could not be further from what I have seen in the schools of Reggio Emilia.

In schools like the one the father described, teachers haven't examined their own thinking about children and about learning. Their understanding has been formed in the US educational system; their underlying beliefs and perspectives are getting in the way of their desire to practice differently. This disconnect directly influences their ability to change the way they work with children.

Although I call what I do "Reggio-inspired practice," it is really an examination of American schools and what teachers do within them. It is about moving beyond one static and culturally bounded example (the schools in Reggio Emilia, Italy) to examine how teachers think about teaching. How does the child learn? This is probably the most important question surrounding twenty-first-century education. Imagine what American schools might be like if they had a different view of children and learning and the role they play in society.

American Education

We have a problem with American public education: it is not working. We can refer to any number of metrics that indicate the stagnation within our primary and secondary educational institutions: high dropout rates, low literacy rates, deep student and teacher dissatisfaction, bullying—the list goes on.

Only in postsecondary education has the United States led the world, measured in both quality and outcomes. There are surely political and economic forces at work defining the striking difference between the primary and secondary failure and the postsecondary success of schools. One thing we cannot ignore: the United States is capable of providing a world-class education, but only for some. How do we widen the net to include a larger group of students who can become equipped to flourish, rather than simply function?

Let us start to answer that question by looking at a few key American ideas about teaching and learning.

Can You Do This?

In 2013, one daily edition of the *New York Times* contains as much content as the average person living in the 1700s would encounter in an entire lifetime. Yet US schools have become increasingly committed to a specific, predetermined set of curricula, tasks, and standards that students must master. With content growing daily and exponentially, it is a futile effort on the part of schools to try to keep up with all of the emerging content being developed. Instead, they need to focus on skills to interrogate, judge, evaluate, calculate, and analyze. The content and dated design of instruction and interactions are falling short of what students in an innovative society need to know and be able to do.

An example of this problem is the standard question that frames most, if not all, evaluations and reports of progress in schools. We ask students, Can you do this? For example, we ask, Can you do the following?

- Count to five or ten or a hundred.
- Recognize red, blue, or yellow.
- Write the alphabet.
- Tell me what this word means.
- Spell this word accurately.
- Label this drawing of a dissected frog.

This type of question can best be answered through multiple-choice questions and standardized measures, but it is not a good assessment of children's capabilities or learning. This focus on content displays the American educational system's conception of the learner as soaking up information without substantially understanding it or connecting it to other knowledge. Indeed, we often refer to children as "sponges"!

Advanced Content, Younger Children

Over the last forty years, American educational systems have consistently pushed content down into lower and lower grades. For example, forty years ago, kindergarten was not mandatory in most school districts. It wasn't even universally available. The curriculum in kindergarten classes focused on helping children learn how to act in group learning settings. Children colored, read stories, sang, played house, did art projects—kindergarten looked a lot like today's preschool programs. Today, most kindergartens are much more structured and much more focused on direct instruction of academic tasks like recognizing and forming letters and numbers.

A similar process has taken place with academic content in all grades, where children are expected (for example) to read and do math at ever younger ages.

Student Engagement and Retention

Student engagement is perhaps the most alarming aspect of our educational system. Students are dropping out of high school at tremendous rates. Each year, approximately 1.2 million students fail to graduate from high school, more than half of whom are from minority groups. Nationally, about 71 percent of all students graduate from high school on time with a regular diploma, but barely half of African American and Hispanic students earn diplomas with their peers. Ninth grade serves as a bottleneck for many students who begin their freshman year only to find that their academic skills are insufficient for high school–level work.

Mental Agility

It is time to ask difficult questions not only about how American learning is structured but about what exactly students need to learn. American schools are not adequately preparing students for their futures, at least in part because school authorities cannot even anticipate what their future will be in order to prepare students appropriately for it.

We live in an age when content is always growing, so what people need is mental agility rather than to master a specific set of content. In our ever-shifting world of innovation, there simply is no link between much of the content our schools insist that children master and lifelong success.

Mental agility and problem solving, of course, are much more difficult to observe and assess than content mastery. But it is mental agility that will enable students to gain mastery of their interests and intellectual pursuits outside of a prescribed curriculum.

The dialogue around what is not working in American schools has been well traversed. It does not serve our purposes to dwell upon it here. Instead, I hope to illuminate what is clear to many practitioners in schools: things are not working as well as they could, and this is in many ways a systemic failure. At the same time, individual teachers can reflect on what they are currently doing and ask questions of themselves in order to move to a place that is more authentically reflective of what they believe schools and learning can be, regardless of the systemic issues. Helping you to begin or continue that process is one of the goals of this book.

I have visited many schools over the course of my professional life. Some of them have an incredible aesthetic: attention to light, beautiful outdoor spaces, rich, textured furnishings and materials. But many of them are still missing something. They may be implementing prescribed curricula that, day after day, try to teach children to write who are not developmentally ready or ask children to group straws into fives and count them as part of prescribed calendar activities. They may have lesson plans focused on animals and colors. When they teach art, they often use a teacher-made model for children to replicate that might, for instance, involve popsicle sticks and cotton balls.

This is not a criticism of teachers, who work hard and do their best by children. It is more a critique of the American educational stance. These projects are the things teachers offer children because this is what they were offered or what they have seen offered and done for years, or even what they were taught to offer children in preservice and in-service education. In reality, children are capable of much more than teachers think, and the offerings are often just scratching the surface of what is possible.

This book cannot answer the larger questions about the educational landscape in the United States, but it can help teachers of the youngest children make changes so that their programs take advantage of educational research about how learning happens, so that students can be well-situated to learn throughout their lives.

How Can Reggio Help?

Reggio-inspired teaching, unlike much of current American education, dovetails with what we know about how children (and people in general) learn best. Using Reggio-inspired thinking and practice, teachers can lay a foundation that will serve students as they move through the system and help them find their own way as learners.

Reggio is about slow, steady engagement with children, involving wonder and joy, as well as questioning and uncovering the ways children construct meaning in their world. The Reggio approach combines the work of important educational theorists like Lev Vygotsky, Maria Montessori, and John Dewey. Schools around the world, including those in the United States, contain the possibility of exploring and integrating the practices of Reggio, along with Reggio ideas about teaching and learning. Educators have the opportunity to create something that works in their school if they start from these ideas about children and apply them to their own work and culture.

Reggio-inspired education is instinctively and aesthetically attractive to teachers and other adults. It is also in line with current research and knowledge about how children learn. Research shows that there is no such thing as a tabula rasa or "empty slate" where children's minds are concerned. Children come to school with knowledge, questions, and experiences. The research of Noam Chomsky at MIT tells us that as humans our brains have an innate predisposition to learn language, which he calls the "language acquisition device," or LAD (1965). Similarly, Elizabeth Spelke and Katherine Kinzler at Harvard University have demonstrated through their research on infants that human brains are predisposed to learn numeracy and geometry (2007). For this reason, language, numeracy, and geometry have come to be known as core knowledge systems. In line with these theories, Reggio-inspired education assumes that children come to school with capabilities and are able to create their own understandings through their exploration and experiences.

Changing the Way Teachers See Children

Perhaps the most fundamental shift that can occur in your practice is to change the way you look at schooling in the life of the young child. Throughout my practice in the past nine years, this has proven to be the most powerful way to align word and deed: examine what you really believe. Remember that education is nestled in culture. What you believe about children is evident in all of the choices you make.

In addition to reframing the questions you ask about learning, you can develop a new idea of what it means to teach or instruct. If schools can no longer focus on teaching content to students in the form of discrete bits of knowledge, how do teachers go about equipping their students with the skills to think and question, in order to transfer those thinking skills, concepts, and tools to multiple settings and subject matters?

Since the publication of *Working in the Reggio Way*, I have had the good fortune to work with literally thousands of teachers across the United States and Canada. The questions that emerge are very much the same across settings. Sometimes when I am listening to teachers, I hear myself in their words and voices. They are asking the same questions I asked as I sat in a chair outside the atelier at Scuola dell'infanzia Pablo Neruda. It's clear to me now that the answers reveal themselves slowly, incrementally. As you engage in the habit of reflecting and questioning more deeply, things you did not and probably could not see at the beginning become visible.

Let me give you an example. I asked participants to bring with them a number of photos from their programs to the first class of a series I taught on documentation. We laid these photos out on a table and looked at them together, set by set, setting by setting. One set showed children who had been given red, yellow, black, and white paint, along with sticks, paintbrushes, and surfaces to paint on.

I remembered first doing documentation with Mara, the *atelierista*, and Patrizia, one of the teachers I worked with. When I looked at the photos, I wanted to tell the chronological story. Patrizia and Mara saw patterns in the children's explorations.

When I did this activity with my own students, they also began to tell the story of the children. They were interested in what should happen next, already focused on moving the process along to the next iteration of what it could be.

When I looked at the photos, I saw two patterns. The students were exploring both color and tools. When I asked my adult students what patterns they saw, the simple shift in framing helped them to uncover a new way of seeing what was in front of them. They also identified the two explorations with color and tools.

The process of learning and teaching in an emergent context is like a ping-pong game with students and teachers taking turns hitting the ball back and forth. In this context, I asked the students what their next move would be. All four of the students had the same knee-jerk response: to introduce more colors and more implements for the students to explore. I suggested doing the opposite and removing everything but the paint, to give students the opportunity to really explore the mixing of the colors.

Sue, the teacher who brought the photos, agreed to try this experiment. The next week, everyone brought photos of what had happened since we had last met. Sue had removed the tools and covered a table with plastic, thereby making the table itself the surface students worked on instead of sheets of paper. In her photos we saw that the students' own bodies, their hands and arms, became the tools. Because Sue pushed the boundaries by offering the children less, the students were engaged in a deep level of exploration that they would otherwise have missed. It was a powerful experience for all of us in shifting our perspectives to see things we were previously unable to see.

Dora, a participant in one of my online classes, was a seasoned and traditional teacher who was interested in making changes to her teaching. Her first question was, "If I am observing a child and see that they cannot do something correctly, then do I develop a project about that for the whole class?" I appreciated Dora's interest and honesty, and I answered her questions with some other questions to ponder. What makes a teacher think that a child could not do something or did it wrong? What if instead the teacher assumes that the child is doing it "right" and proceeds from there? What question is the child trying to answer?

This is where culture rears its head and asks us to make choices. American education is concerned with doing things "right" and getting the "correct" answer—solving the problem for the child instead of engaging with them on the journey of figuring it out. Reggio-inspired education is more concerned with what the child is thinking, exploring, or wondering and how to support their experimentation so that it is deeper and more thorough.

What Can You Do?

In Reggio Emilia, teachers understand learning as anchored to personal experience, from which all theories grow. All experience is personal; each person's understanding of the world is filtered through experience. This does not mean that all understandings and theories are negotiable. But it does make learning personal and autobiographical. This personal experience includes theories and hypotheses about the world within larger conceptions of culture in the classroom, school, and community. Picture the child at the center of circles like bowls nested inside another. If children are learning a new concept in an outer bowl, it needs to be attached to understandings that exist within the learner, in the central bowl.

This perspective asks for a fundamental shift, which comes from one simple question that Reggio teachers ask. Instead of "Can you do this?" which implies that there is a correct answer and a content-specific response that all children should have learned, teachers ask, "What can you do?" This question puts the child at the center of the learning and values their own knowledge and experience. Through posing this question and looking at how children talk about and display what they know, we can determine what is happening in their minds. This is much more interesting than determining the facts they know, because it is linked to critical thinking.

Reggio teachers understand that when they are working with children, accompanying them on their journey to make meaning out of their world, it is the children's meaning to make; teachers are simply along for the ride. Superimposing the teacher's beliefs and understandings does not really support the development of children's ability to figure stuff out. In Reggio-inspired education, teachers honor children's perspectives—not as exclusive but as necessary to the conversation.

For example, if your students seem to veer off on tangents when they try to answer a question, ask them how their thoughts—or their long and rambling stories—connect to the topic at hand. Just because you cannot see the association does not mean it is not there. Get them to share their perspectives; it might change how you think about what they're learning.

Open-Ended Curriculum

In Reggio Emilia, curriculum is largely open-ended; that is, it doesn't have a predetermined result or destination. This is another way in which curriculum in Reggio supports what we know about how children learn. Research tells us that young children's learning progresses from simple to complex and is embedded in their own lives and interests. This calls for curriculum with many options and activities that are open-ended without a clear resolution or outcome, or at least not a predetermined one.

An open-ended curriculum provides a lot of repetition. It allows children to do something as many times as they want to, as many times as it is interesting or satisfying for them, without a predetermined "end" decided by the teacher. Children like what they like, and when they like something, they like it a whole lot, time after time. This is why they want to hear the same book, see the same movies, and tell the same jokes again and again—they love to hear the same stories over and over and over.

I can remember a story my grandmother used to tell when I was a child about when she traveled to Mexico with my grandfather. They had been feeling sick but were avoiding drinking the tap water. Wondering where to get water they could drink safely, they called the front desk, and they were told they could get bottled water from their hotel room's minibar—something entirely new to them. My grandmother laughed about how she and my grandfather hadn't known the solution was right in the room. I know the story by heart—I heard it many times—but I loved hearing it each time as much as my grandmother loved telling it.

It's human nature to want to repeat enjoyable experiences over and over. It's especially true of young children.

Nonlinear Instruction

Reggio Emilia teachers put the child at the center of learning, paying attention to how they learn and what they are interested in rather than focusing on whether they are meeting standardized milestones. Research tells us that learning happens in a nonlinear fashion, that it cannot be tied to a timeline or placed in an absolute sequence. Each student meets materials and builds knowledge along their own unique path. This is why readiness checklists tied to decontextualized learning are not an appropriate way to assess children's development or learning.

One day, at Pablo Neruda, one of the three-year-olds, Lucrezia, was eating her lunch. As I sat down next to her, she looked at me and asked, "Julie, are you going to stay in Italy?" I told her I didn't know; I was not sure how long I would be there. She continued, "If you stay, you should probably learn to speak Italian." (We were, in fact, having this exchange in Italian.) I thought about this for a moment and asked her, "Lucrezia, do you speak English?" She paused and said no. "Well," I continued, "if you do not speak English and I do not speak Italian, how are we communicating?" Lucrezia looked at me and continued to eat, mulling the question over. It would seem that because my American accent was so thick when I spoke Italian, Lucrezia thought the different pronunciation was another language. This was the theory about language and communication that she had constructed as a three-year-old with her life experience. This was the place to begin to build on her theory and interest. My question was genuine; I wanted to know what her ideas were.

This exchange highlighted the connections Lucrezia was making based on her observations and interactions with the world. Lucrezia may have been the only one in the class who thought I was speaking English, or there might have been others. This exchange was an opportunity to begin an exploration together—she and I and maybe some of her classmates. The principles of language acquisition and second-language learning were not something I would naturally think of discussing with a three-year-old. However, in a very natural way, she had posited a theory that she had about the world. This presented me with an opportunity to help her test, stretch, and revise this theory as part of our time together.

Being open and attentive to these kinds of moments and the learning they embody will not be found on any readiness checklist. However, the ability to ask questions, formulate theories, and test them serves Lucrezia (and any student) for years to come. As the teacher in that moment, I had a choice to recognize the opportunity and seize it without knowing where it would take us, how it might unfold, or what would be accomplished—or I could brush it aside. Being open and attentive to these kinds of moments and to the learning they embody is essential to teaching in the Reggio way.

Changing Your Practice

I am often asked for the quickest way to change practice. Americans tend to want an easy solution! I can appreciate that. I have frequently sought the simplest solution to problems for a long time. If you intend to change the way you look at teaching and learning, the best way to do this is regular written observations of students and regular reflection on this process. You must find your own way, using your observation of students and practices of Reggio Emilia as a place to start. You can apply Reggio ways of thinking and doing with children in your American cultural context, rather than trying to make your program look on the surface like a Reggio school.

Making these changes is an incremental process that the schools of Reggio began after World War II, sixty years ago. Give yourself some time. Remember that the work happens incrementally. There are no quick routes to changing how we see the world.

I think that most teachers would want to seize the moment in an exchange like the one I had with Lucrezia above, but they are not sure how to do it. In order to recognize and take advantage of these opportunities with children, you need at least three things: to recognize the moment, to know how to move from the moment into a more extended exploration, and to have confidence that if you depart from your habitual ways of teaching, it will all be okay.

First comes recognizing the significant conversations and moments so that you are able to seize them and engage the children. That takes practice and time. The best way to start is with the question I've already mentioned: What can you do? In the case of Lucrezia above, "What can you do?" translated as "What do you think about this?" Instead of telling her that I was speaking Italian already and explaining *my* theory to her (that she mistook my heavy American accent for a different language), I asked her what she thought was going on. Use the "Reflect and Connect" sections at the end of each chapter, and your journal, to help yourself ask more and better questions of your students and give them fewer answers.

Second, you'll need help knowing how to scaffold a conversation into the next one and then the next one and how to incorporate it into the documentation and involvement of other students. See especially chapter 4 on *assemblea* and the pedagogy of listening.

Last, but maybe most important, is the confidence that if you veer from the prescribed format, and start to make changes to your practice, the children will be okay, and the classroom will still function. And I promise you, they will be okay. You may have to try it out to see this for yourself, but I'm confident that if you do, you will be serving the children you work with.

Reflect and Connect

Start this journey with examining your intentions
for your practice and your professional growth. It will help
engage your ability to reflect, skills you will refine
throughout this book.

- In your journal take a few moments to describe where
  you are right now as a professional—struggling, growing,
  challenged? You are the only one who will read this, so be
  as honest as you can about what you are doing well and
  where you are challenged and would like to grow.
- Next, keep your eyes open for two kinds of things in the
  next couple of weeks to write about: the things you are
  doing well and the opportunities that present themselves
  for you to learn from. It might be easiest to take a few
  minutes at the end of each day to jot these down in a
  couple of columns. You will see that no matter what you
  said about where you are, you are already doing things
  that you feel good about and are likely successful at
  doing. And you are lucky enough to still have challenges
  that will lead you to improving your skills.
- Finally, write down where you would like to see yourself
  at the end of this book. What changes are you hoping
  to make? What is one area where you would like to see
  progress?

Onward to the real work now.

Creativity seems to emerge from multiple experiences, coupled with a well-supported development of personal resources, including a sense of freedom to venture beyond the known.

—Loris Malaguzzi in *The Hundred Languages of Children*

Chapter 2

Sopratutto

Tenets of
Reggio-Inspired
Practice

The word *sopratutto* sums up this chapter very nicely—in Italian, it means "overall." The principles in this chapter are the things that stood out to me thematically overall about my experience in the schools of Reggio Emilia, Italy. To make it easier to discuss them, I've made a list, but they are not discrete concepts operating in isolation. In some ways these practices can serve as connective tissue for other elements of education.

In this chapter I discuss the critical elements of what I observed in Reggio Emilia about the experience for children from birth to six years old. These themes arose from qualitative research methods. After many months of review, I condensed the thousand pages of notes on my observations in Reggio Emilia into one page of themes. I continue to organize my written work based on these notes. As an American doing research in the Reggio schools, with a foot in both cultures, I used these reference points to guide decisions about my work and to illuminate a clearer understanding of what a Reggio-inspired approach could be. When I'm working with teachers and programs who are exploring Reggio-inspired teaching and learning, I frequently return to these same themes to inform my interactions with schools and teachers.

This is not a template; the ideas are dynamic, and each program brings them to life uniquely. However, each idea is part of the larger tapestry of Reggio teaching and learning. These ideas link other, more familiar curricular elements of a Reggio-inspired approach, including documentation, projects, the environment, and children's participation, among others. These are the ideas we'll explore in this chapter:

- There is no "pre" school, as there is no "pre" life.
- The child is the protagonist.
- Children's developing agency must be supported.
- Teachers do not say no "just because."
- The environment is the third teacher.
- Teachers work in the same ways they ask children to work.

There Is No "Pre" School,
as There Is No "Pre" Life

When I arrived at Pablo Neruda on my first day, Mara Davoli, the *atelierista*, greeted me in the lobby and took me on a tour of the school. She told me stories of Loris Malaguzzi, the father of the Reggio approach, that still resonate today as critical to understanding Reggio-inspired practice. Malaguzzi believed that schools for young children should be called "schools of childhood," not "preschools," because they were not preparing students for anything else. Instead, they were appropriate places for children at the ages they attended. The learning and experiences that happened in the schools were not geared toward some other day in the future; rather, they were important and relevant as they were.

Malaguzzi likened the work and learning in the schools of Reggio to filling the pockets of the children with coins they could spend later. The idea was to create an ever-increasing wealth of strategies with which children could engage the world. Similarly, the schools used real-life implements instead of toy tools. For example, in Reggio glass vessels are used in school. It is common to see baby food jars used in the atelier to mix paints. At lunch children eat with ceramic dishware, use knives, and drink out of glasses rather than plastic tumblers. Children are trusted with typical daily materials from their homes. Children are usually experienced with the materials, and if they are not, their experiences are scaffolded to afford them the opportunity to learn.

For example, one day when I was working with the three-year-olds, there were simply too many children (twenty-six of them) for three adults to cut all of the meat that was served at lunch. So we asked who knew how to cut, and we gave them knives. Then we started showing the other children how to cut their meat into pieces. We moved around the table both cutting and showing, which proved to be a useful and efficient way to build capacity in the kids in a safe setting. I could not have imagined something that would seem out of place in other settings unfolding in such a natural and intuitive manner. The other option was for the adults to cut the food of all twenty-six kids, keeping many of them waiting a long time to eat.

Children also had the opportunity to take apart machinery like radios or unused VCRs. They loved the chance to use tools like screwdrivers to take out screws and wires. Many students returned to this project day after day. When I was working with a school in New York, we brought in an old stereo receiver. For a few weeks we watched, full of wonder, as the children marveled, puzzled, and approached this device. They wore goggles and moved around it, exploring different aspects each day. The three-year-olds who worked on this project participated in both parallel and collaborative play. Sometimes they would show each other what they found or ask if they could try a tool that someone else had. The teachers were able to gather many artifacts by introducing everyday objects into class.

I have also seen hammers and nails used for projects when warranted. Learning how to think about and make sense of the world requires real experiences. And building real experiences requires exposure to real tools.

The Child Is the Protagonist

The "protagonist" is the main character in a story, the one the story is about. In Reggio, many people refer to an educational triad—student, teacher, and parent—constructed with the child at the apex and the parent and teacher in roles supporting the child. The idea that the child is the protagonist of the classroom is that the educational experience overall—this story in the classroom—is about the child and their interests, explorations, theories, and questions.

Children are the protagonists in a Reggio-inspired classroom, but this does not mean that the children are the only characters in the story. They have teachers and parents and siblings and classmates, all of whom are characters in the story and support and develop the protagonist. Similarly, school activities are designed around children, but children are not there alone. The structure of the school holds them and allows them to engage deeply in exploration. Perhaps a better way to conceive of the child as protagonist is to picture them in the center of the nested bowls described in the previous chapter.

In many conversations I have heard in American schools, I have noticed the common misunderstanding that "The child is the protagonist" means that the child is the ruler in the classroom. That is, the program should follow the interests of the children and leave aside the expertise and guidance from the teacher and other adults, who play passive roles. This is a literal and limited view of the concept.

Beneath the idea of the child as protagonist there is an *intento proget-tuale*, or "intended projects," in Reggio, a structure that is largely invisible to children and often also missed by outsiders. It is a rich structure that works like the frame of a house being built. It is supported by the Reggio environment acting as the third teacher and by the *assemblea* or morning meeting, which lays out the options for children and frames the thinking and hypotheses involved. In Reggio schools, following the children occurs in a well-defined setting that has been developed over time by adults with expertise. This structure encodes the knowledge and experience of more than sixty years of working with children in this way, even though the *intento progettuale* is not made explicit.

American teachers are often working without this framework, without the knowledge encoded in these structures (*intento progettuale*, environment, *assemblea*) that have been developed over years of practice. Teachers can't just adopt the framework of Reggio Emilia; they have to build this structure painstakingly for their own programs and cultural context. Most teachers don't have concrete guidance in creating a school experience and structure that enable them to follow the child. Without this structure, American programs can and do become chaotic, with children who either run wild, grow listless, or both, lacking structure and scaffolds to support their exploration. This is not the idea behind "The child is the protagonist."

Children's Developing Agency Must Be Supported

"Agency" means a person's independent ability to act on their desires. One of the most important goals of any educational program is to help children develop agency. Children struggle with decision making, self-control, and other forms of agency, and schools are the perfect place to develop those skills. When we think of young children, we often think of the need for impulse control and the ability to recognize cause and effect. But in fact those skills come much later in their development. Instead, it's crucial to support the ability of young children to have a voice and act on their emerging agency. Then later, at age-appropriate times, self-control and recognition of cause and effect will emerge.

It seems obvious that children should act on their desires, but it is actually a learned skill. Learning to manage agency is rooted in the ability to recognize and act on what you want. For example, if a child wants a friend, agency might mean overcoming shyness and rejection, as well as developing strategies and language to make friends.

When children are three, four, five, or even six, learning the way this happens and how to act on their own desires should be natural. However, in many early childhood programs, teachers are so busy asking children to do what they are told that it minimizes children's ability to develop agency. This contributes to larger problems in the lives of children because having agency leads to the development of self-control. It seems paradoxical, but doing what adults tell them to do does not help children learn self-control. Being able to understand, express, and act on what they want develops children's thinking skills and control over their free will. This is why attention to and discussion of agency is central to the implementation of an effective early learning program.

Developing agency in a child is related to the idea of following the interests of the child, in that it takes place with limits and within a structure. Structure informs a child's sense of agency and can determine or limit it and his or her decisions. However, we are so busy asking children to do what we tell them that it minimizes their ability to develop agency. In Reggio, one child I knew, Fabio, was totally overwhelmed by the many choices he had when he arrived at Pablo Neruda. Over time, he calmed down and learned to manage his interests and the time he spent on each of them daily. His teachers, Paola and Patrizia, said that in fact they had seen this situation often and that when children were given choice for the first time it could be overwhelming. But it was better for Fabio and the other children to learn to manage their time and interests than for them to wait to be told what to do their entire lives. We have all likely seen individuals at varying ages who needed direction. In a child it is understandable; in an adult it can be problematic. Without the freedom to choose, or without a scaffold in place to support this choice, it would likely have taken much longer for Fabio to learn to manage his interests, if he had done so at all.

Ideally all early childhood experiences are assisting young children in developing agency. A Reggio-inspired program begins by helping children to develop agency—with appropriate guidance and boundaries—and builds from there.

Many teachers have questions about what happens when students transition to elementary school. My friend Ivana had two sons at Scuola dell'infanzia Diana. She told me, laughing, that when her boys transitioned to elementary school, they were immediately proposing projects, voicing interests, and exerting their agency all over their new classrooms. Their teachers had to learn how to harness the agency the students brought with them!

Teachers Do Not Say No "Just Because"

When I lived in Reggio Emilia, I taught English to an eight-year-old, Giovanni, once a week for three years. Giovanni had attended Scuola dell'infanzia Diana, and his mother, Margherita, told me a story from Giovanni's time at Diana. For a period of time when he was four, Giovanni liked to dress up in costumes—different ones everyday. When he went back to school from summer vacation, Margherita thought that the costumes would disrupt class and that surely the teachers would tell her this was unacceptable for school. She was surprised when they arrived at the school and the teachers instead said, *Vediamo* ("We'll see"). The teachers explained to the family that they took students as they were. The teachers were not going to make the behavior an issue until a problem presented itself.

This is a different way of positioning the school and the child from what is often seen in American preschools. It avoids anticipating problems and thereby creating them before they exist. It goes counter to American fears of lawsuits and to American licensing requirements, but if we want to look at what is best for learners, a bit of calculated risk and doing the extra work to offer possibilities for children can result in big payoffs.

Many years ago, when I had just returned from Reggio Emilia, I consulted in a classroom for one- to two-year-olds, where I found the resource choices to be surprising. There was a book rack with books whose pages had been ripped and were generally tattered. All of the good books were stored up in cabinets that were bolted to the walls far from little hands and where the children could not get to them.

I asked why the good books were put away and was told that they might get ripped like the others. Well, of course they will! I thought. You teach children not to rip books by giving them books and communicating how they are handled and what value is placed on them.

This change was resisted by the teachers. "But what if . . .," they said. "What if the children did not rip the books? What if they instead loved and cared for the books?" I said. The teachers would never know unless they got the books out of the locked cabinet and put them in the kids' hands.

On a more personal note, when I was growing up with four siblings very close to me in age, my two stepbrothers and I were somewhat obsessed with fire—well, with matches. We would take many books of matches from the drawer in the kitchen, go and sit outside of the backyard gate on the cement path alongside the garage, and light them. Sometimes we would light one or two at a time and watch them burn, holding them until we were about to get burned and then throwing them into the dirt next to the house. Sometimes we would light whole books at once and watch them go up in flames. In retrospect, we are lucky we did not burn the house down.

Children are naturally curious about fire, and had there been a place for us to safely explore fire it would likely have been better for all parties involved. But we knew the answer would be no, and in a classroom it would also likely be no—but why? Just because it seems dangerous? Or because the adults cannot be bothered to get permission, set up something safe, and get into it with the students?

The Environment Is the Third Teacher

In Reggio Emilia, schools for three- to six-year-olds have twenty-six children and two teachers per class. This means that both teachers are just that: classroom teachers. The environment is a critical part of the invisible structure that enables teachers to follow the children's interests. The environment can display intentionality and both ignite and enhance projects that students engage in.

As the third teacher, the environment can cultivate children's ability to engage and teachers' ability to observe and respond to learners who are living and creating their experience. Through the environment, the teachers put materials and places at the disposal of the children, who fuel their own stories ("the child as protagonist").

In *Working in the Reggio Way*, I shared stories about what I called "self-managed projects." For example, there were wire clouds on a table that children could engage with at their own pace as well as opportunities to weave with yarn, which was set up on the floor on a large, wooden frame. These opportunities created by the teachers are one example of the environment as the third teacher. The students were in a position to engage the environment, the materials, and even the projects without adult intervention. The environment itself served as an intermediary. Self-managed projects are one way that the two ideas of projects and the environment intersect in Reggio.

Other examples of the environment as the third teacher include the games area and the construction or house play area. All of these are clear sections of the classroom, and they are also part of how the environment and the projects included in it support the students' autonomy and choice. As the third teacher, the environment also supports children's developing agency.

Teachers Work in the Same Ways They Ask Children to Work

In American early childhood programs, teachers often think of themselves as the ones with the answers. Teachers are taught that it's their responsibility to know the children's developmental stage, to assess their readiness for school, and to plan what children should be learning. In Reggio Emilia, teachers work in the same cycle of inquiry that they support in the children's work: they observe carefully, they ask questions and develop theories, and then they experiment and observe again to see the results of their experiments. The teachers as well as the children are viewed as learners in the context of the school.

For example, Paola and Patrizia, with whom I worked closely at Scuola dell'infanzia Pablo Neruda, were not satisfied with how children were using the construction area of the four-year-olds' classroom. Through observation, Patrizia and Paola saw that girls in the class used the space minimally and that the periods of time the children were playing in the space were shorter than the teachers had observed with past groups.

As learners themselves, they began a project to understand more clearly what was happening in that area, using an informal dialogue they had developed in ten years of working together. Instead of assuming they knew what wasn't working, or trying things without a clear purpose, they asked themselves questions in a cycle of inquiry to hypothesize about what the children would respond to, and then they observed children in the space. This was the same way they guided the work of students: asking questions, observing, hypothesizing about possible avenues, and then testing these hypotheses.

Paola and Patrizia theorized that changing the character of the environment—in this case, by projecting nature images on a nearby wall—might invite a different kind of engagement from the children. They set up a slide projector to display the images, covering a space of about four feet by three feet; this did indeed change how children used the area. More girls were drawn to the area, the children played there for longer periods of time, and their constructions took on a vertical dimension the teachers had not seen before.

This is just one of many examples of the teacher as inquirer that played out parallel to the projects that unfolded with the children in the classroom. Here's another: When I was working in the five-year-olds' classroom, Antonia, a master teacher and questioner, would use the students' queries to fuel her own projects as well. Once some students came running to Antonia, saying, "He hit me!" Antonia used this as the impetus to explore the process of relationships in the classroom. While the students were sorting out being offended, making it right, and the crimes and punishments involved, Antonia took a thirty-thousand-foot view and asked herself and the children questions like these: What would you like me to do? What are the appropriate punishments to be meted out? Who decides, and who punishes? In this way she was able to contextualize her students' learning in the larger world of human development as well as continue to refine her own skills as a reflective, questioning professional.

Using the Ideas

Think of these six ideas as some of the threads woven throughout day-to-day life in a Reggio-inspired early childhood program. Some of these will emerge daily, as central to the practices in Reggio. Others are part of the teachers' vision or overall philosophy. In Reggio Emilia the ideas function in an interconnected way that is sometimes invisible to outsiders, but calling all of them out concretely is helpful to our exploration of Reggio-inspired practice.

It is less like a simple list than like one large ball of yarn. All of these concepts are related to and support one another. The process of not saying no leads to building agency, and the environment as the third teacher is part of the approach to projects. Both teachers and students develop in the schools of Reggio Emilia. It is all connected.

Reflect and Connect

Consider your own teaching and learning practice.

- Think about your journey as an educator. What are your greatest challenges in your practice at this time? List those here or in your journal.
- Which of the six ideas do you find most interesting? Which seem the most mysterious or puzzling? In what ways?
- How have you already explored these ideas in your work with children? How does your work relate to these main concepts?
- Which would you recommend to a colleague as the most important to understand and fold into their practice? Try placing them in priority order. Where would you start?
- How might you like to grow in relation to these areas? Write down your ideas. For instance, is there an opportunity for you to stop saying no "just because"? Perhaps you want to develop a project or some questions of your own. What are you investigating in the classroom? It might even be that you want to approach your environment differently or more critically.

If we are to become more effective teachers, we need to become more reflective teachers. To be reflective we need to articulate our theories of learning, critically examine them and replace those parts, which we suspect or, better still can show, do not work.

—John Dewey, *How We Think*

Chapter 3

American Challenges

This chapter shifts from the overarching view of Reggio-inspired principles in chapter 2 to a closer examination of Reggio principles as they are understood in American culture. We'll examine the way that Reggio-inspired practice shifts in the translation from Italy to the United States and the influence of the cultural context of the two settings.

Americans have been gazing longingly at the schools of Reggio Emilia for decades. Many attempts have been made to export or replicate the practices the schools have developed. But there is no kit to buy that will enable a school to authentically call itself Reggio-inspired. There are some aspects of Reggio practice, however, that carry more weight in building momentum for the beginning of the journey. What makes a school Reggio-inspired is related to behaviors and practices that teachers and students choose to engage in. This is where the Reggio-inspired life dwells. It is not only related to the sophisticated aesthetic found in Reggio schools or the evolved documentation panels—what are typically identified in the United States as key parts of Reggio. These things matter, but they make visible the practices of inquiry, reflection, and collaboration embedded in the work of Reggio-inspired teachers and students.

There are significant cultural differences between the schools of Reggio Emilia, Italy, and schools in other cultures that are interested in working in Reggio-inspired ways. The culture within which a school is situated has a definitive influence on the internal culture of the program. This is true for all three components of the educational triad: parents, students, and teachers. In the American context, for example, the implementation of Reggio-inspired ideas is notably influenced by licensing requirements and safety concerns, which don't exist in the same way in Italy. Similarly, parental pressure toward outcomes and achievement stems from US societal norms; parents' concerns are a significant part of US culture and quite different from the Italian culture of Reggio Emilia. These are just two examples.

In the United States, these cultural conditions contribute to restrictive experiences that leave little time for children to explore their interests and construct their own knowledge. It's typical in US programs to have many discussions about time on task, centers, overly organized and scheduled days, prereading and premath exercises presented out of context, and so on. Educational programs are asking students to learn in ways that are driven by the culture within which the programs reside. The larger culture also creates the microculture within the school. In this chapter, we'll discuss some of these cultural influences and the thinking behind them, and suggest some work-arounds to help you align your views on learning and schooling with your daily practice.

Exploring Culture: Americanisms and Misnomers

Over the last decade, it has become crystal clear to me that all things are culturally rooted. More and more, this idea permeates my stance as an educator, and it infuses this book. The more I live and travel, the more I notice how the systems within a culture—justice, education, business—are all imbued with its values, whether or not those values are explicit. Both educational experiences, generally, and the development of schools for young children, specifically, are influenced by culture. This is especially important when looking at the success and construction of an educational system.

One of the biggest difficulties in bringing Reggio principles to US programs is the difference in the way the same ideas are conceived of and acted on in the two cultures. Once pointed out, the patterns of disconnection discussed in this chapter seem quite obvious, although they may not be so easily identified independent of a discussion like the one here. Think of an optical illusion or puzzle that baffles you until the solution is revealed, at which point it seems intuitive or simple. Culture functions similarly.

This chapter explores common realities of American schools that are often overlooked when schools are trying to change their practices, and Reggio thinking that is often misinterpreted in the translation from Italian culture to American society. These misinterpretations do not necessarily damage children, but they limit and stifle them, while compromising their opportunities for learning and thinking that the program or teacher is offering them. Teachers' experiences are also limited. Over time, students realize that institutions like schools will eventually mold them into a model of what the institution desires. I do not want to contribute to that process on young minds, and neither do most teachers. And it begins with culture.

American Cultural Barriers

When I work with teachers on Reggio-inspired practice, the conversation consistently circles back to culture. Many times, teachers want to say that many educational practices, especially environmental ones (e.g., tablecloths, open snack, indirect lighting versus fluorescent), are not possible for Americans because the practices are embedded within Italian culture and an automatic part of the surroundings in Italy or Europe in general. But I believe that it is possible to create these settings for children and that it can be done in the United States—except for the barriers we face culturally.

In one group I worked with, one teacher in particular was very defensive about the images we shared and discussed. Again and again, she focused on the images as evidence that because the schools were in Italy, the settings were not possible for American programs. It was true that the images were from Italy and came out of Italian culture. However, the opportunity that she resisted was that of looking at her own practice and the possibility of rendering a more refined and reflective space for children within her school and classroom, taking small steps.

This dismissal of the entire project as too large or too grand is something I have seen both in my work years ago as an interpreter for international delegations at Reggio Children and more concretely since my return to the United States. It represents people's resistance to the complexities of change. Change happens through a consistent effort over time—not in one fell swoop and not in a few days or weeks or months. The need for immediate measurable results—a common American cultural tendency—somehow supersedes the process of cultivating successful, lasting change. But we must remember: either we build culture, or it builds itself.

School Culture

Everything that takes place in schools influences the experience of the students. Schools are intrinsically organized as social places with learning at the center, and learning is a social activity (Zins, Bloodworth, Weissberg, and Walberg 2004). Research has shown that schools will heighten both their success as institutions and the immediate and long-term success of students when they prioritize efforts to integrate children's academic, social, and emotional learning (Elias et al. 1997).

School culture is the set of norms, values and beliefs, rituals and ceremonies, symbols and stories that make up the "persona" of the school. Recall the image of nested bowls from chapter 1: the smallest is the child, nested in the classroom, nested within the school, nested within the city, within the state, and then within the larger national context. Unwritten expectations build up over time, as teachers, administrators, parents, and students work together, solve problems, deal with challenges, and, at times, cope with failures.

For example, every school has a set of expectations about what can be discussed at staff meetings, what constitutes good teaching techniques, how willing the staff is to change, and the importance of staff development (Deal and Peterson 1999). Schools also have rituals and ceremonies—communal events to celebrate success, to provide closure during collective transitions, and to recognize contributions to the school. School cultures also include symbols and stories that communicate core values, reinforce the mission, and build a shared sense of commitment. Symbols are an outward sign of inward values. Stories are group representations of history and meaning. This is true of both the classroom culture and the whole school culture. In positive cultures, these features reinforce learning, commitment, and motivation, and they are consistent with the school's vision.

Elements of Cultural Disconnect

Here are the most common elements of cultural disconnect related to Reggio-inspired practice or aspects of our American culture that limit our ability to get inside Reggio-inspired practices.

- Adding a mirror triangle is not enough.
- Development is nonlinear.
- Emergent curriculum is not free play.
- Following the child means "It depends."
- Children having more freedom is not a bad thing.
- Rules do not solve problems.
- Licensing is not an excuse.
- Reflection drives planning.

Adding a Mirror Triangle
Is Not Enough

Typically in my online classes, each week I ask students to send me photos of whatever we are working on and upload them to share during the online class with the rest of the students. One of my students, David, was new to the Reggio approach. He proudly shared his photos showing the changes he was making in his program.

As I listened to him and looked at the images, I was struck once again by the focus on the objects in the space, which was being created without student interaction. It wasn't new or unique to David. Many teachers feel intense pressure to add a light table or a mirror triangle; they don't think about how to integrate these into the experience, and they don't make a connection to the children's explorations or interests at the time. Simply adding a mirror triangle or a light table does not make a program "Reggio-inspired."

In Reggio

In Reggio, the elements of the environment came together in a much more organic and collaborative experience, whether at Pablo Neruda, Nido Bellelli, or any of the other schools I visited. A dance between students and teachers unfolds within the lived environment just as it does within the curriculum. The process of changing the environment is inclusive of the children and happens step by step. As with the curriculum, it includes back-and-forth dialogue of try, test, revise and is based on observation and reflection.

Ideas for You

I would encourage you to look at your environment and making changes to it as part of a process, rather than seeking a destination. You can use the process as an opportunity to further engage your students and their families by soliciting feedback and incorporating varying perspectives. Perhaps most importantly, give yourself permission to evolve and understand your space and the needs it serves over time. When you move into a new place, you need to live there attentively for awhile with the other inhabitants before making big, irreversible changes. Not having one particular item (a couch, for instance) does not mean that it's not a home. Similarly, in the classroom, live attentively for awhile with your students. Adding or passing on a mirror triangle or any other piece of equipment is not the definitive element in your program becoming Reggio-inspired. It is much more about what is happening in the space than about any furniture placed there.

Development Is Nonlinear

One of the greatest fallacies that dominates education is the connection most people have to their own education. We tend to think that what we did and how we did it in our own schooling was how it should be done. In fact, with evolving research on the brain and human development, we have much more information about the most effective ways for people to learn and therefore what good schooling should look like. Further, early childhood education has become common only in the last twenty to thirty years, and many of us may not have even attended preschool. So we are anchored to a skewed reference point. We are doing what has always been done and not necessarily what is effective or developmentally appropriate. Couple this with the ridiculous marketing to young children and their parents and caregivers, which pushes colored plastic, ABCs, and, 1, 2, 3s, and you have a recipe for ineffective education. These overly simplified concepts are limited in comparison to what young children's complex and highly functioning brains are capable of doing. Dr. Alison Gopnik, author of *The Philosophical Baby*, recently described infancy in these terms: it is like being in love while in Paris after having had three double espressos. That is how alive and active the young brain is. And yet we offer "red, yellow, blue," "A, B, C, . . . 1, 2, 3, . . ." "train, boat, car" . . . We have not understood the full realm of possibility in teaching young children.

In addition to potential that is beyond what teachers and parents expect, all children learn along unique timelines and not always in the same sequence. We learn to ride bikes at different times, walk at different ages, and speak at different times and in different ways. Some babies start with single words, and others don't say anything until they can speak in sentences. This continues to unfold with relationships, jobs, everything in their lives. We must abandon the idea that children will unfold in an orderly fashion, one that is easy to check against a list.

Ask yourself, do you see young children as capable and competent? Do you see them as individuals, each bringing something unique to the conversation? Ask yourself these questions—even if not aloud—and then think about what you say you believe and the way this is lived in your classroom. To engage this process of reflection frequently is a serious and transformative challenge.

It's important to constantly reflect on the messages we are presented by marketers. For example, the question "Can baby read?" The larger question is not "Can baby read?" but "Why does baby need to read?" Baby has plenty of time to read. If baby can "read," they probably are decoding but not comprehending. This skill is only moderately useful and not worth the trade-offs needed to acquire it. The bottom line is that baby will read when baby is ready. But baby may be four, or seven, or even nine years old before that happens. They will figure out when and how, and it will look different for each of them.

In Reggio

Students are viewed so differently in Italy than in the United States that it is even a difficult comparison to make. I think that the pressure on parents to help their children have opportunities begins very early on and intensely in the United States. I clearly remember from the years I lived in Italy how children and childhood were embraced as a unique and valued part of life. Children were certainly coddled and nurtured, often extending the period of childhood. But there is something beneficial in a childhood that is not measured by accomplishment or achievement, and in which the individual development of each child as it unfolds is not only allowed but embraced.

Ideas for You

In order to take a step back and embrace the notion that development is nonlinear, it may be helpful to actually build segments of time into your program that guarantee you are able to slow down. Think of these times to slow down as speed bumps in your busy day. Stop what you are doing, and spend five minutes simply observing what is happening in that moment.

Emergent Curriculum Is Not Free Play

Another common misconception about situating the child as the protagonist within the classroom and setting up an emergent curriculum is the idea that this means there is no structure and that it is a free-for-all in which materials are put out and children come and play freely without direction. This is simply not the case. Emergent curriculum requires intentionality on the part of the educator.

This is a powerful and dynamic relationship, based on the concept of ping-pong questioning. The teacher hits the ball to the students (this may be a *provocazione*, a conversation, a question), and as the teacher observes the students' response, information is collected and synthesized with hypothesizing taking place about what the children are doing and are interested in. Then the "ball" is reshaped and hit back to the students—and so on.

In Reggio

Reggio involves a highly choreographed structure, invisible to the outside eye, that has been added, layer by layer, week by week, and through interactions with all members of the educational triad (parents, students, and teachers). Settings seeking to embrace Reggio-inspired practices most often miss the crucial concept of intentionality. At the heart of the difference between "emergent" and "free" is the idea of intentionality. Behind every *provocazione*, each offering and question, are ideas and questions on the part of the teacher about what the students are doing, how they are developing, and what might further this development along. The next chapter further discusses intentionality, but putting out materials and leaving the children to explore these without the back-and-forth interaction and dance dynamic can only go so far.

Ideas for You

Intention is addressed in greater detail in the next chapter, which will further assist you in honing in on this concept and your intentions as they relate to your setting. As a first step, ask yourself a few overarching questions: What do you want the daily experience to offer your students? This can be on a macro level—for example, at the end of the year, what would you like them to remember? In addition, use weekly and daily check-ins with yourself and your colleagues to decide the intended flavor of the day. This will help you make choices about what you will offer your students and how you will offer it, and it will help build this capability in your practice.

Following the Child Means "It Depends"

I have given the same response to so many questions, but it is consistently the best answer: It depends. It depends on the teacher and the context and the day in question. Each choice made in a project or conversation or construction of a panel of documentation is a one-time choice. There are patterns that emerge in individuals and groups, but there is not a rule or way to predict the outcome of any particular endeavor. This idea asks for a certain degree of comfort with chaos that may occur. It asks for a recognition that events and development do not unfold in entirely predictable ways.

In the United States, we like more concrete and surefire responses to questions. But becoming comfortable in the unknown, in the flexible and uncertain, will continue to push us to be better and to do better. Humans adapt quickly, and that is often why our practice can become rote and unimaginative. I've had those moments in my own professional experience. With pressure to be one step ahead of the answers, we sometimes stop asking questions. Questions about our views, our students, and what is happening in our classrooms are critical to keep our practice fresh and vibrant. Teachers at their best function as researchers, and research is all about questions.

In Reggio

Within the Reggio approach, no one is looking for the one correct answer. Choices are understood to hold true for one setting, with one set of teacher and children, at one time. At the same time, the choices and decisions align with larger values, which are understood and shared by the educators. American educators don't yet have this clear shared understanding that is reflected in their work with children. Becoming comfortable with the ambiguity of "it depends" is the next stop on the journey as Americans work to define and integrate these concepts into their educational culture.

Ideas for You

The biggest idea and probably most effective one I have is to relax. I think about all of the new teachers I have worked with and how earnest and diligent they are. They make commitments and promises and break their backs to keep them. Relax! Learning is lifelong, and we have time to keep trying. If you can slow down, pause, and give yourself time to respond to what is happening in front of you, to reflect on what the children are doing and be open to new ideas, you might just find that things will blossom in directions you never anticipated.

Children Having More Freedom Is Not a Bad Thing

One of the overriding elements of American schools is the attempt to control student behavior and choice. We live in a litigious society, which often prevents us from giving children the freedom to explore, make mistakes, and figure things out for themselves. But this freedom is the foundation of lifelong learning.

I can recall a number of power struggles in my time as a classroom teacher that did not move me or my students any closer to a positive and engaged learning experience. I am reminded of this every time I go into a classroom and in every workshop. The behavior I see—being right, having the last word, and getting your way—is much more about controlling every aspect of the classroom. This is not aligned with any successful educational vision. Let's take a few steps back and examine how this manifests, what the thinking behind it might be, and how to move away from control into comfortable freedom.

What is the role of an educator in the lives of their young students? In a traditional American model, teachers are the ones who lead, decide, poke, prod, encourage, organize, and are essentially situated at the center of the classroom and therefore educational experience of their students. This model of education is what we have likely each experienced and been taught in our own preparation, not to mention the expectations of schools and administrators to continue to do what we know and understand. But let me advance another model of what teaching and the role of the teacher can be.

In Reggio

I can remember when I first started at Pablo Neruda, I was a wreck. Even though I had been teaching for a number of years, I was literally sweating with worry at the amount of freedom the children enjoyed. It took some time to realize that it was a well organized and well thought-out design. It was not chaos. It was intentional and thoughtful. The students knew their options and their limits, even though of course they challenged them constantly. The noise level never became unbearable. One of the noticeable differences from American programs was the lack of teacher direction and what I can only call "interruption" of student learning. In many American settings all eyes are on the teacher. It is a kind of *protagonismo*: the teacher as protagonist. In Reggio this kind of teacher direction was noticeably absent. The students were the protagonists. This difference correlates directly to the way in which American teachers interact with students, or at times even drive and control student choices and behavior.

Ideas for You

In one of my classes, a teacher talked about a recent experience in her program. When it was time to clean up and go outside, the students did not immediately respond to her announcement. She said that normally she would have reminded them of her request, as she expected them to respond immediately when she changed the tone or direction of the class. But this time she stopped herself from reminding them. She told us that she simply watched as they took their time cleaning up and moving outside. It took about ten minutes instead of two. But, as she described it, it was so much easier and less dramatic.

This metacognitive act, in which the teacher reflected on her practice, is what enabled her to change it. I challenge you to pay particular attention to what and how you are asking your students to do. Is it happening in the way you want? Why is this what you are most comfortable with? How can you create a pause in your default request and give students a little more room to breathe and decide?

Rules Do Not Solve Problems

Linked directly to the struggle for control is the presence of rules in the classroom. American schools have rules for everything—how students sit, what they do with their hands, how they line up, how they go to the bathroom, and on and on and on.

The licensing rules intended to create minimum standards of quality for child care are linked to programs' rules for children. Teachers ask me about how to strike a balance with licensing guidelines such as hand washing, or keeping thirty-six inches between mats during naptime, or . . . The list goes on.

There are tensions between what we want to do in our classrooms and the legal parameters we're required to follow. Between state licensing guidelines and guidelines from the National Association for the Education of Young Children, setting up an experience that reflects what we believe about children and what they deserve can be challenging. Think for a moment about the one guideline that you are asked to follow that makes the least amount of sense to you.

Now think back to some of the overarching tenets of Reggio practice explored in the last chapter. Remember "Teachers do not say no 'just because'"? This issue about rules is a good place to apply that principle. Can you move beyond saying no "just because" to embracing yes? Just as we must shift from "Can you do this?" to "What can you do?" we must also change from anticipating reasons not to do something to beginning with the idea of "Let's see" and continuing with "We'll work it out." I have watched teachers tell students, "Do not do that," or "Get down from there," or simply "No no no." I find this imposition of the teacher's desires on young children disturbing. Rules do not solve problems; they limit experiences. How can you embrace the possibility in things that you do not know, things you are not sure of, and things that make you uncomfortable?

In Reggio

In Reggio, rules were addressed differently in different situations. One thing I noticed is that there were not a lot of arbitrary rules front-loaded at the beginning of the school year. Instead the rules emerged out of a demonstrated need or situation.

Ideas for You

What would happen if you could and would negotiate the rules with students as the needs emerged, and with each group a bit differently? You could continue to refine your own practice over time by revisiting the same conversation periodically with a new group of children. It's much like working on and questioning the environment after the students have arrived, and with their input. The idea of "emergent" as key to being Reggio-inspired could apply to many aspects—as many as you can tolerate—of the school experience.

The idea of getting to yes will be challenging for many reasons, but it will benefit you and your students and the entire daily experience. The payoff for the work will be enormous. This might mean brainstorming on the things you want to change. This may also mean collaborating with a colleague and having a trusted coworker watch you teach and ask you about what they see. If you are particularly brave, you may actually open the conversation to your students. If they are three and a half or older, they may be able to tell you what they like and what could be improved.

Licensing Is Not an Excuse

All too often in my talks with teachers, licensing guidelines are presented as limiting the possibilities for schools to be inspired by the environments and practices in Reggio. I bring this up not to criticize licensing as a problem in and of itself, but rather to point out the way teachers use guidelines as a reason not to change their own practice. This is especially apparent when we look at photos from programs in the United States and images from Reggio. Teachers too easily dismiss the potential of the Italian images based on the licensing limitations in the United States. For example, when looking at a photo of the mattresses that the children set up next to each other to sleep on in Reggio, I have often heard teachers say, "We can't do that because of licensing regulations." This is an easy way to dismiss the onus for reinterpreting our realities in better ways that are more respectful of young children. Teachers easily see change as not possible since things cannot be done exactly as they are in Reggio.

Remember that Reggio programs did not begin where they are today. They have faced and overcome challenges in their history as well. Licensing limitations are challenges to be innovative and creative while balancing the needs of the children with state guidelines. This is where critical thinking and the ability to cultivate multiple solutions to a problem need to be developed so that the work is engaging and the solutions dynamic. This is where options about hanging things or using wall space or glass mean that you need to ask yourself what is interesting and engaging for children and not simply the path of least resistance. The guidelines from licensing agencies have been written with intentions that are more protective than educative for children, and that is where the role of the teacher as interpreter comes into play.

In Reggio

When I was working in the Reggio schools, there were no heavy licensing requirements that measured such arbitrary things as square feet per child and distance between napping mats. It is important to underscore that the licensing requirements should not be seen as impediments to offering children the best experience possible. These challenge us more than ever to look for solutions and not simply resign ourselves to a less than stellar educational experience simply because licensing makes things difficult.

Ideas for You

Think carefully about your "musts" (if this concept is unfamiliar, see chapter 3 of *Working in the Reggio Way*). What is most important to you in terms of the way you structure your day and environment? Which battles are you willing to fight? I am unwilling to step back from what is best for children, even if at times it is in opposition to licensing guidelines. Do we really want to ask young children to lie on mats at least thirty-six inches from another human, when we know how scared and vulnerable one can feel when falling asleep? I don't think this is in the best interests of young children. If I were a classroom teacher, that would likely be the battle I might choose. What is your battle? Instead of using licensing regulations as an excuse not to change, ask yourself what you really want your students to have, and then go to bat for it. Dialogue with the licensing agency and research to support the decisions you make are paramount in creating the experiences you desire for your students.

Reflection Drives Planning

Reflection—the ability to look at your work and yourself as well as the work of others—is an important activity to use in your practice. Reflection means more than checking things off a list or looking at a lesson plan. It means thinking about how things went, what worked well, what did not, what tweaks could be made, how did the process feel, and how did the students respond. It is peeling back the initial layer, which is experience, and unpacking the deeper feelings and thoughts that lie underneath. There are many expert sources on how to develop and improve reflection, but the first step is to reserve the time to engage in reflective practice. Reflection happens during and after an activity, and for many teachers this does not feel natural. Teachers are taught to plan forward instead of to reflect while they are in the process and then adapt what is happening or going to happen in response to this reflection.

This is the difference between, on the one hand, planning for what is coming next and, on the other, reflecting on what has happened and using this reflection to inform next steps and choices. Picture a number line from 1 to 10, and imagine you are standing on the number 3 facing toward the 10. Planning in the American education system is a matter of constantly looking forward toward the 10 and planning ways to get there. In Reggio there is a more dynamic action of looking back toward the 1 and using this to inform your path as you move toward the 10. Instead of a straight unidirectional line, it is more like bobbing and weaving. All of this is done while interacting with students and reflecting on the process.

The number line is a simple image that cannot fully represent the action and dynamism that needs to be taking place within teacher practice.

Nevertheless, it can serve as a visual aid to further the conceptualization of Reggio-inspired practice.

In Reggio

While I was in Reggio, the idea of teachers looking critically at their own and one another's practice was an intuitive and implicit activity. The process of reflection was literally embedded in the day-to-day life of the Italian schools. Teachers would discuss things on the fly, while they were talking to students during *assemblea*, taking notes, and conferring with each other and the students at the same time. There were also more formal meetings in which the whole staff would look at projects in process and discuss them. Teachers were having reflective conversations with themselves and one another throughout the day.

Ideas for You

The best way to begin incorporating reflection in your practice is to use a journal. What first needs to change is your internal process. You want to form a habit of looking forward and looking backward all at once—of looking at your work, talking about it, taking notes on it, thinking about it. This is all part of the reflective process: to turn things over and over and see them from varying angles. Think of the number line, and imagine yourself standing at the 5. Instead of planning along all the way to the 10, you want to look backward to what has happened (at 1, for example), and pay attention to what is happening right now, and move forward slowly based on those reflections.

Reflect and Connect

- Which concepts discussed in this chapter resonated with you? Why? Name at least two examples of how you see them in your classroom or program.

- Next, think about ways you would like to make changes, and write about them. Think about why the concepts you noticed are rooted in the culture in which your school exists. How did you come to embrace them? Asking yourself these questions will enable you to take the necessary steps to move from where you are to where you would like to go.

Our task, regarding creativity, is to help children climb their own mountains, as high as possible. No one can do more.

—Loris Malaguzzi in *The Hundred Languages of Children*

Chapter 4

Assemblea and the Pedagogy of Listening

From the last chapter's thirty-thousand-foot view of American challenges with a Reggio-inspired approach, we are going to come down to earth and look at one central component of the approach, that of *assemblea*, up close. This discussion will be broken into conceptual concerns and practical considerations, all of which must be addressed in order to construct a workable American Reggio-inspired program. I will highlight skills and strategies that form part of Reggio schools' daily life. Making these explicit will help you tease them out of the Reggio program and think about how to use them in your own setting.

This chapter looks at the heart of a Reggio-inspired educational program: *assemblea*. This is the same period of time called "circle time" or "morning meeting" in many American early childhood programs, although the pedagogy is often different in the United States from that of *assemblea*. During *assemblea*, ideas and theories are expressed in conversations that give shape to projects. Here children let Reggio teachers inside their thinking; students are asked for their opinions and are engaged in dialogue. Thus *assemblea* creates a platform for students to express and build knowledge. The teacher's purpose is less to assess or evaluate children's knowledge on a particular topic or to elicit a certain "right" set of answers than it is to understand what the children are thinking or wondering.

American teachers have frequently told me about challenges surrounding circle or meeting times in their classrooms. Tension often surrounds the efforts made to control children or the amount of time children are expected to participate. In most American schools, circle time is planned with games and songs and a great deal of routinization. These activities are usually divorced from the other activities during the rest of the day, falling far short of what could be done and gained from the time together. When there is conversation, the teacher's purpose is often to introduce a particular, concrete topic that she has determined is important or to evaluate what the children know about a topic.

In the morning, the children are fresh—their thinking is clear, and their language is also likely at its best. This is why scholars insist that professionals and workers should do their best and most important work first thing in the day. In thinking about morning meeting, ask yourself: What is the most important work of the day in an early childhood program? In Reggio, it is talking to the children and hearing what is on their minds—where their interests are and what connections they have made to the work of the previous days, weeks, or even months, and then building a day or project to further this exploration. Reggio teachers do this in *assemblea*, in the morning, because that is when everyone is at their best.

The difference between *assemblea* and meeting time resides largely in pedagogical differences between Reggio and American schools. One way of understanding Reggio pedagogy, and *assemblea*, is as a "pedagogy of listening."

Pedagogy of Listening

Teachers in Reggio Emilia consider the child to be the carrier of theories, interpretations, and questions. Instead of the teacher transferring knowledge to the children, Reggio-inspired teaching sees the child as the protagonist and co-constructor in the process of building knowledge. One of the biggest challenges to American teachers in Reggio-inspired programs is to embody this idea instead of simply giving it lip service. Reggio teachers have had sixty years to experiment with this idea and get closer and closer to putting it into practice. For most American teachers, this is a new idea; they are steeped in an educational tradition that defines teaching as the conveying of knowledge from the teacher to the children.

If a teacher believes that the child constructs their own knowledge, then the most important verb that guides the educational activity is no longer "to speak," "to explain," or "to transmit," but rather "to listen." The only way teachers can discover a child's questions, theories, or interpretations is to listen to them—to listen to what they say aloud and to the many other ways that they convey their ideas. This is the pedagogy behind *assemblea*.

Carlina Rinaldi has helpful insights about the role of listening in education. Listening means one person being available to another who has something to say—available enough to hear them with all of the listener's senses. Listening is not simply registering the message but also interpreting it. The message acquires meaning and significance at the moment in which listening captures and validates it. Listening legitimizes the one who is speaking because communication gives form to thought. When someone is listening, the thoughts of the speaker are at the center of the interaction, the reason for the connection. In the case of teaching young children, listening to them makes the children the center of the interaction—the protagonist.

In an early childhood program and specifically in *assemblea*, the teachers are invited to create a favorable context in which children's curiosity, theories, and research can be legitimized and listened to. This is a context in which children feel at ease, motivated, and esteemed while they are pursuing their own processes essential to knowing. Teachers also get a peek into the inner workings of the children as individuals and as a collective. If teachers were scientists, this would be their time in the lab. And trying to do scientific experimentation without observation of the experiments and participants is unthinkable.

The role of the teacher is distinguished by listening, observation, documentation, interpretation, and continued hypothesizing of possibilities developed by the *progetto educativo* (educational project). Another primary component of a teacher's work—and therefore the work of the school—is to help each child "learn to learn." This kind of school is like a construction site, where the processes of the children and adults actively cross paths and are evolving every day.

The pedagogy of listening is at the heart of an effective *assemblea*. As in all other student-teacher interactions in the Reggio approach, a pedagogy of listening during *assemblea* is essential as a reciprocal action in which the listening both informs and validates.

Shifting from talking to listening—from leading to accompanying—is a significant repositioning of the teacher's and the student's roles. Listening to children makes it possible for teachers to engage in the ping-pong rhythm of learning, listening, collecting information, and synthesizing, and then offering witness, hypotheses, and understandings back to the children for their response. Again, in this dialogue the children are the protagonists.

Intention

Until several years into my Reggio exploration, I did not understand intention and the weight it could bear on the work of a teacher and the happenings in the classroom. There are at least three kinds of intention in an early childhood classroom: the teachers' intention, the students' individual intentions, and the broader intention of the group as a whole—the experience of what is happening and what is being thought and acted on. When you see how many intentions there are in the room, it's clear that the teacher's intention is central, but only one part of the whole.

The teacher's intention is their thoughts and desires about what is to be constructed and experienced by the children. The teacher's intention touches the experience of each student, since the teacher becomes the facilitator and is involved in every project in some way. I was thinking about this riding the bus in New York City recently. One of the stated goals of American society is equal opportunity for its citizens. This intention is expressed in the structures that are developed for the citizenry. The bus I was riding had a route developed to support this desired intention. This kind of intention can be built into schools and classrooms as well. When you think carefully about the experience you would like to create for your students, when you are aware of your intention, you can build systems to support your overall learning and experiential goals. This is the concept behind *intento progettuale*.

In a Reggio-inspired program, although a teacher has an overarching intention about what might take place in the classroom, they cannot drive or determine the ultimate direction of any quest that students undertake. There is a magic place—uncharted territory—between intention and manifestation. A teacher may have hopes and intentions for their students, but the children may meet the teacher with something else or may lead the teacher to a surprise. This is where intention and the pedagogy of listening connect. Without listening to the children, a teacher cannot discover the children's intention.

Ideas that are central to Reggio pedagogy—learning in fits and starts, planting seeds that need time to germinate and come to fruition, the need for ideas and learning to incubate—are often unfamiliar to American educators. In my classes for teachers, some of them want to go forward, move more quickly, and make connections, when clearly other individuals in the group are not ready. This same dynamic happens in early childhood classrooms when teachers superimpose a timeline for children's learning based on their timeline for teaching (the scope and sequence, or a planned curriculum). This is an example of expecting one intention (the teacher's) to override all the other intentions in the classroom.

As part of my graduate school program I served as an adjunct professor at Columbia Teachers College, where I observed and mentored student teachers from the early childhood program in their placements. The student teachers worked in a variety of schools, so I was able to see a broad spectrum of early childhood settings, including some that identified themselves as Reggio-inspired. I can recall a couple of times I witnessed morning meetings going terribly awry.

One classroom in East Harlem was filled with robust and polite students. I came in and sat in the back of the room just as the student teacher was asking students to sit on designated spots in the circle. That was the first thing that caught my attention: students had little carpet squares that delineated where they sat and how much space they could take up. This was a way for the teachers to prevent squabbles, but it took away the opportunity to learn. Why not give students the chance to build interpersonal skills in a safe place?

The meeting progressed with calendar activities that were part of a purchased curriculum, and the student teacher followed the script. It involved counting straws for the number of days that had passed and then grouping these into fives and tens. It was not an entirely useless activity, but the students were wiggly, and the teacher was doing most of the talking. The culmination of the morning meeting was when the teacher led the students in a rendition of a song by the popular hip-hop artist Jay-Z. She had them follow along and sing the words as she pointed to the lyrics on a poster board. These children were not yet reading, but I could see that she was trying something inventive to match lyrics and words they knew to printed words on the page. Children began to jump up and dance, and the whole experience crumbled before her eyes. She had structured the experience to scaffold their sight-word development. She hoped that linking the printed words to a song they knew would have an effect of accelerating the lightbulb moment in these children: they would recognize that the words they heard were also the words they saw on the paper. That was her pedagogical goal. The goal of the teacher education program was for her to demonstrate she could control the children in a group. Once they got up and danced, she had clearly not achieved the goals of the exercise for her as learner—to control the children in a group—although there were certainly other ways to look at the experience.

In this teacher's defense, she was a student, and this is not an unusual group-time experience. She had clearly worked hard on preparing the materials, and she had a clear intention for the group. But there was no space in her design of the morning meeting for the children themselves—for their ideas, for their curiosity, for their reactions to what she was introducing. The teacher's intention was primary, and there was no room for her to listen to the children and discover what their intentions might be.

On another day I went to what was considered to be a model progressive school in New York City to observe one of my sharpest and most thoughtful student teachers. She and I had discussed morning meetings versus *assemblea*, and she was really interested in meaningful classroom experiences. When I arrived, I sat on the floor with the students, and this situation was the polar opposite of the one described above. In this case, the students were in charge in a way that did not benefit them. The teacher was having difficulty getting the attention of the whole room to read a book, as they were following their own interests—which meant anything from poking each other to talking loudly to hitting. The student teacher was trying to get through the book and keep control of the most restless students by asking them to sit beside her, but it was a futile battle. The notion that she would be able to deliver anything intentional while the students had free rein was impossible.

I am sure that you have seen or participated in morning meetings that looked just like both of these. Unfortunately, neither extreme is unusual in American programs. Here's a different example from Reggio. This example of *assemblea* illuminates the questioning patter, ping-ponging, and use of inquiry with children, asking questions and reasoning through theories they have. This positions the children and their ideas at the center of the conversation, creating their hypotheses and supporting them in actively seeking and constructing knowledge.

In this example from the five-year-old classroom at Neruda, the child is positioned as the protagonist, with the teacher listening to the children as they hypothesize and think their way through a query. Antonia, the teacher, is reflecting back to her students her understanding—what she hears and comprehends.

"Come in, Julie." Antonia greets me at the door. The children are excited because we had spent several months together when I worked in their class earlier in the year. After our greetings, the children and Antonia quickly settle back into what they were doing before I arrived.

"Okay—the question. Let's ask Julie if she can help us." Antonia looks at me and continues, "If we usually have twenty-six children, and today there are twenty-one, how can we determine how many students are missing?"

Silence follows while the five- and six-year-old children wait to see if I can answer the question their teacher posed.

"Hmmm, tough question," I respond, looking at Antonia and following her lead.

"Yes, it is," Antonia agrees. Then, addressing the entire group, she asks, "Does anyone have the answer?"

Illaria and Matilde raise their hands indicating they have already figured out what math operation will solve the problem. They tend to find answers immediately and usually before the rest of the children in the group.

"Okay," Antonia tells them. "But you two stay quiet. Who can offer a hint to the others?"

Elisa indicates that she is ready to help her classmates solve the problem. She says, "I would count all of the children and then count all of the chairs and see which of the chairs remain empty. This way I can figure it out."

Andrea chimes in, "But that wouldn't work."

Antonia responds, "But Andrea, we are asking for other ideas, not criticism of the ideas so far. Daniele, do you have an idea?"

"No," Daniele, a shy boy, answers.

Antonia continues around the circle of chairs, inviting each child to contribute. "Guido, do you have a suggestion?" she asks.

"No," Guido responds.

Antonia continues to give each child an opportunity to share ideas or suggestions that could help their friends answer the question. Carlotta offers, "I would count all the names of the children—who is here and which names remain. This way we would be able to figure it out."

Antonia turns to Alice and asks, "Which method would you prefer?"

"Elisa's," Alice says.

Antonia continues, "What was Elisa's method?"

Alice hesitates a moment, "Count the children."

Antonia "Then . . ."

Alice, "Count the chairs."

"Which ones?"

"The empty ones."

"*Brava*," says Antonia, satisfied with the discussion and that Alice is following it. She looks around at the students and begins again.

"Roberto, how would you do it? Like Elisa or Carlotta, or in another way?"

"Like Elisa," Roberto says.

Antonia goes on, "Let's try. I will tell you what the number could be. Using your systems, let's see if we can figure out the actual number."

Antonia whispers something to each child. When she gets to me, I too want to hear the secret: "We are missing five children."

Then Antonia asks Carlotta to get a piece of paper and a pen, and Antonia posts the paper on the wall.

"We are how many today?" Antonia asks again.

Carlotta answers, "Twenty-one."

"Okay, write it here," Antonia instructs Carlotta, handing her the pen and indicating a place in the middle of the blank piece of paper.

"Good. Two, then one—right. What is the other number to write?" Antonia asks.

"Twenty-six," the children respond in unison.

"Right, when we are all here, we are twenty-six."

Most of the children gather around the paper on the wall to participate in figuring out the answer to Antonia's question.

"Where do we put the twenty-six?" Antonia asks, turning to Matilde.

Matilde stands up, responding, "Over the twenty-one."

"Right. What operation do we have to do?" Antonia asks.

"Subtraction," Matilde replies.

"That's right: Twenty-six minus twenty-one equals . . ." While Antonia points to the actual problem written on the paper, the children are silent for a long moment as they work to figure out the answer on their own. Some count on their fingers, while others figure it out in their heads.

"Five," a voice calls out, and Carlotta looks to Antonia before writing the answer below the problem.

"Okay, who goes home at one o'clock?" Antonia continues with the daily count to determine who will eat lunch and who will remain for the post-rest snack.

"I do," says Emanuele.

"So," Antonia asks, "what do we do now?"

The children agree to subtract one from the new total to see how many children will remain. They place this number below the twenty-one and subtract again.

"Okay, who wants to take the numbers to the kitchen? Let's talk about our projects for today." Thus Antonia gracefully transitions to the next topic.

After reading about this *assemblea*, take a moment to write down how you would have experienced it as a child who was asked the question. What do you think the children might have been thinking at that time? How would you imagine the children's parents would describe this *assemblea* if they had seen it? What intention do you think Antonia had? Where in the story does she listen to the children? What does she learn?

Antonia was a master at finding the embedded opportunities and knowing how to ask a question just ripe enough with possibility that she could get the students' wheels turning. At this point in the year and the educational experience of the students, her intention was to cultivate problem solving. She also wanted to involve some basic numeracy and computation, as these students would be going to the state-run elementary schools the following year, and it was time for them to at least be introduced to these processes. Antonia listened to the students, heard and validated them, pushed their ideas about how to solve the problem, and took the time to walk them through the scientific method of formulating a hypothesis and testing it as a group. It is a powerful example of *assemblea* and the pedagogy of listening.

Finessing Your Own Circle Time

As you work to move your morning meeting in the direction of a Reggio-inspired *assemblea*, you will want to make incremental changes. Each small change adds to and builds on the one before. Trying to implement all of these ideas, or even several at once, is a mistake. This is your opportunity as a teacher to make one change and then, in the same way that you dance back and forth with the children on other projects, watch the children's response.

Keeping the themes of chapter 2 in mind, use this as an opportunity to build your skills by working in the same way as the children. Think of circle time as your project. Investigate it. Ask the children about it. Make change one step at a time. Watch for the children's response, reflect on this response, and then respond accordingly. If you can conceptualize and feel that rhythm—the back-and-forth of a dance, of a ping-pong game—you will be working toward more Reggio-inspired practices in your classroom.

Here are some possible small changes you can make to your circle or morning meeting:

- Listen to the children.
- Keep circle time short, and expand it in one-minute increments.
- Play with seating arrangements.
- Make sure children are comfortable.
- Consider your rituals.
- Serve food.
- Make it social.
- Involve the children.
- Stop the gimmicks.
- Manage wait time.
- Let the children lead.
- Surprise the children.

Listen to the Children

One of the most difficult things to master is controlling a group of young children. You'll do better if you can relax, instead of constantly trying to drive the discussion and pace of the morning meeting. This means listening to what the children have to say. This approach can change the entire dynamic from reactive to responsive.

This is a good place to start your circle time project. What do you most want to know? What can you ask the children about circle time?

Keep Circle Time Short, and Expand It in One-Minute Increments

Often teachers become frustrated as their students get fidgety and talkative. It is important to have realistic expectations and to manage these expectations actively. Sitting in groups and having many people be at the center of attention is a learned skill. Go slowly, and build the students' ability.

For instance, begin the school year with having a five-minute meeting each day. Add a minute per day or per week, in order to gradually build up the students' expectations and abilities over time.

Play with Seating Arrangements

It's easy for teachers to get stuck on one way of having children sit at circle time—for example, literally in a circle or on carpet squares. Sometimes children like to sit in chairs, sometimes on the floor, sometimes next to the teachers, and sometimes next to friends. Sometimes they like to see everyone, as in a circle, and sometimes they like to be arranged more loosely. Give children different opportunities to experiment with their seating, and you will get different participation and behavior out of your class.

Make Sure Children Are Comfortable

Adults are never asked to sit on the floor for meetings, and this is a difficult arrangement without back support even for young children. Consider these factors when setting up your circle time, so that the structure facilitates success for the participants: Do you need chairs, pillows, back supports? Do all the children have to sit, or can they shift position as necessary?

Consider Your Rituals

Calendar, singing, sharing, storytelling, work planning—there are many common rituals for circle time. In some programs the group counts the children present. In some programs they talk about the weather. What do you do during circle time? Did you inherit these structures? How are they working for you? Are the day-to-day structures, which can tend to clog the meetings, necessary? Are the activities fluid enough to meet your students where they are? What purpose do the activities serve?

It is important to determine the purpose of circle time. One is to see and talk with students. What is your intention for circle? How can your intention lead you in the direction of a pedagogy of listening?

Serve Food

In Reggio Emilia, food is often served at *assemblea* as a unifying gesture. Serving a small piece of fruit is a great way to regularly begin your meetings. Food can support social and community development among your students.

Make It Social

Play games, mix it up with call and response, or use chants. Learning is tied to action for young children. This is a great opportunity to play with your children as well. Guessing games, search and find, puzzles, and word games can be great ways to promote collaboration and thinking skills while keeping things fun and interesting.

Involve the Children

Let the children help plan circle time. Ask them to reflect on what works or why circle time is important. Giving the children a voice in the execution of circle time can help this process evolve and get the children more involved and attentive.

Stop the Gimmicks

Teachers often use gimmicks during circle to attract and hold their students' attention. Gimmicks are attempts at control. They don't work because they harness children's attention in fleeting ways to an external prompt, which is not very interesting in the long run. They are a classic example of *extrinsic* motivation, which comes from outside the child, rather than *intrinsic* motivation, when a child attends because they are genuinely interested and engaged.

For instance, a teacher will use the term "crisscross applesauce" to get children to sit quietly, so she can have their attention, but she can genuinely gain their attention by eliciting their knowledge, asking an interesting question, listening to them, playing with them—the list goes on. Classroom management is not about gimmicks, and depending on them does not develop the craft of teaching. These tricks may work in the short term, but they do not yield long-term benefits.

Manage Wait Time

Silence in the circle is okay. When you are uncomfortable, the same does not always hold true for students. Young children do not have a highly developed sense of time and its passage. When you are sitting in a circle and need to regroup or have lost the direction you wanted to go, you can take a moment to catch your breath.

Let the Children Lead

Giving up control can often restore the balance in a classroom. Sometimes taking the risk of letting children run a meeting—or at least take part in the leadership—can provide a calming effect and an unexpected engagement on the part of all students in the class.

Surprise the Children

The possibility of finding a surprise that could be both thought-provoking and fun is enough to get small children clamoring to get into school in the morning. This method of engagement jump-starts class dialogue, and it is a good tool to have available. Surprises can be linked to parent education; parents can leave materials, constructions, or other artifacts from their school visits for the students to discover.

Use the examples above as a point of reference as you work on your teaching practice. They're not complete—nor could they ever be—but they're a start.

Reflect and Connect

As you think about this chapter,
ask yourself these questions about your practice:

- Are you satisfied with your *assemblea*?
- How do children participate? Do they bring ideas from home? Do they build on each other's stories? Do they ask questions?
- Where do you see your classroom among the chapter's examples of morning meeting?
- What would be your ideal morning meeting? What purpose would it serve? What intention would you hold for it? What would it look like? How would it unfold? Describe it in detail.
- What steps can you take, starting slowly and using the advice from this chapter, to help your morning meetings move closer to Reggio-inspired practice?

Stand aside for a while and leave room for learning, observe carefully what children do, and then, if you have understood well, perhaps teaching will be different from before.

—Loris Malaguzzi in *The Hundred Languages of Children*

Chapter 5

Intento Progettuale

5

Thinking and Learning
in Reggio-Inspired Schools

I have often been asked what is it that makes Reggio schools so special. It is difficult to narrow it down to just one thing, and of course it depends on what each person considers "special." The schools of Reggio Emilia are amazing examples of what schools can be and do—and not only for young children. Wise decisions and choices have been embedded in the design of these schools that educators of children of all ages can learn from.

The children of Reggio Emilia are part of what is special. But so are the teachers and the environments and the cooks and the culture within which they live. For the purposes of our work, let's focus on the children. Imagine a human being who is ready and eager to learn, is able to ask questions and conceptualize projects, can tell you their theories about the world as well as think critically about their own learning and that of their classmates, freely offers solutions and resolves conflicts—in short, participates in learning in a robust and self-directed fashion. This would be a marvelous description of a graduating high school student. But this description can apply to young children. This is what the six-year-olds are like when they leave the Reggio Emilia schools.

It's clear from this outcome that the Reggio approach supports children's development. But what contributes to this outcome? In Reggio Emilia, teachers are not concerned with "readiness" for the next stage of education, but with real problem solving and thinking. Loris Malaguzzi was known to say that the Reggio Emilia schools were not called "preschools" because they were not in preparation for anything else but were right for the children at that point in their development. The Reggio schools are concerned about and built around young children and all that implies. American schools, on the contrary, are consumed with concerns about readiness, regardless of the fact that readiness often cannot be linked to academic success or other kinds of success in later life.

"Readiness" is not even a term that exists in Italian. *Pronti* or *pronto* are the words for "ready" (as in "I am ready to go"), and it is how Italians answer the phone, but a *pronti*-ness simply does not exist. In Reggio the emphasis is not on a list of skills but instead on a child who is participating in the learning process, unimpeded by adults' choices in the design of the educational program or by the interactions between adults and children. Reggio students are products of this stance: mentally agile, precocious, engaging, vibrant, proposing and attempting to actualize their own hypotheses. Beyond simply offering ideas, they want to test and wrestle with them. This is what an active, engaged learner looks like at any age.

But What About Academics?

It's all very well to aim at the engaged, competent, eager learner we described above, you may be thinking, but what about academic skills? How do children learn how to read in Reggio Emilia? How do they learn how to count? The question to ask yourself is this: What approach to reading and numeracy is precisely tailored to these early childhood years? In Reggio, reading, numeracy, and other concepts that we would think of as "academic" are aimed at children in the moment, not in the future. They are embedded in the day-to-day life of schools and learning, in much the same way that they are in our own lives as adults. You learn to do certain things because they present themselves to you in context and they are useful and interesting. For young children, most things are interesting, and competency feels good. We have all seen a child who has proudly mastered a new skill, be it reading or counting. They do not need to be forced to do these things—they have an innate desire to learn. It is how people are hard-wired.

Think for a moment about literacy and numeracy in your life. Adults do not typically schedule times to exercise these skills. We use our calculators to find the balances in our bank accounts and plan for trips and purchases; we read as part of daily life—street signs, instructions on recipe cards, magazines and books and websites. According to current research, American adults have so wholly embedded these acts of reading and writing in their lives that they are virtually seamlessly integrated with their daily activities.

This is how we should think about learning in the schools of Reggio. Opportunities for children to encounter "academic" skills are conceived in advance through the *intento progettuale*. Other opportunities to support the development of these skills are seized when they emerge. Teachers continue to build the scaffold children will need as their lives demand ever-increasing fluency with these skills, but the skills themselves are integrated into day-to-day life. That context helps children learn.

Intento Progettuale

My first exposure to the *intento progettuale* was well into my first year at Scuola dell'infanzia Pablo Neruda. I can remember in the first weeks marveling at the daily details of the school, the way the whole experience was enacted by the teachers and students as if it were a choreographed dance in which each partner knew what to do. This was unlike anything I had ever seen, and I looked for the plan, the outline, the script that made it all possible. There wasn't one. But there was a road map, which anticipated the projects that teachers knew, from a combination of experience and knowledge of early childhood, would come to pass in the school lives of their students from three to six years old. In Reggio schools, the children stay together with the same pair of teachers for three years, so it is highly likely that an outline of anticipated and therefore intended projects (*intento progettuale*) will come to pass over the course of that time.

The *intento progettuale* include topics that all children encounter, like these:

- the process of relationships
- *segnalibro* or "bookmarker"
- self-identity
- color

Intento progettuale also includes other subjects that are situational by school, by group of teachers, and by the group of children as they move through the school, but this list of four could be considered the foundation for examining topics that teachers are certain will arrive in the lives of children, based on the teachers' experience and knowledge of child development. Think about these themes as being in a kind of parentheses that a teacher can insert in anticipation of an experience. For example, experience and knowledge of child development tells the teachers that there will come a time when children are caught telling a lie. This forms an opportunity to explore more deeply the topic of honesty or not telling lies. Teachers may have some thoughts beforehand about the topic, things they want children to experience or think about, but they hold those thoughts in parentheses until the opportunity comes about to explore them.

Similarly, teachers in Reggio insert these kinds of parentheses into their thinking about the classroom experience in anticipation of moments of natural development to arrive. As you consider them, you will think of other possible *intento progettuale* for your own setting. Sharing, eating, self-soothing—these might be appropriate for your school and students.

The intended projects provide the road map to a place the teachers and children are visiting, with a list of things they think they might encounter along the way. The purpose of the *intento progettuale* is to help the teachers anticipate the journey.

On the wall in the entryway at Pablo Neruda are documentation panels that serve as a snapshot of the projects happening in each classroom. These are mainly taken from the *intento progettuale*, since they are long-standing and enduring. The long timeline offers the time and space for children and teachers to develop these projects and subsequent documentation panels, which also serve as the calling card of the school. It is the first thing visitors see upon entering the school.

The teachers collaboratively decide in advance which of these projects will likely present themselves as opportunities within the early childhood experience, and when the conversation or event that could give birth to a project occurs, the teachers are ready. Since they know they are looking for a way into these projects, they are more ready to identify the opportunities when they present themselves.

This is both a complex and encouraging thought. By talking to colleagues and through the collective intelligence of the crowd—the wisdom of experience coupled with a knowledge of child development—teachers can accurately anticipate what will emerge in a group of three-, four-, or five-year-old children. The time, place, and context for the project ideas within *intento progettuale* are undetermined, and therefore all of the other interesting things that emerge as short- or long-term projects still have space to emerge, while the teachers also keep in mind the *intento progettuale* and look for the moments when the project ideas may show up.

Intento progettuale is a way of thinking about curriculum, and it can be learned. The dynamic and open-ended nature of this kind of thinking is the key to enacting the Reggio approach.

Intento progettuale also supports the Reggio emphasis on problem solving and thinking in the moment. Teachers can anticipate where student agency may lead by virtue of their own experience, and they are ready to meet it when it arrives. This is like a giant, invisible safety net. It enables the teachers to collaborate, reflecting on past experience and using this to project what might come to pass with their students.

Questioning

In *Working in the Reggio Way* I described ping-pong questioning, in which questions are not answered but instead a back-and-forth exchange between teacher and student occurs. Children's questions are typically answered with another question. This helps the child understand or interrogate their own theories about the topic. By asking a question, the child is indicating they already have a theory about the answer. The pedagogical goal is to help tease that out instead of supplying an answer. How questions are answered is representative of the way children are understood to be engaged in learning.

Questioning develops a mind-set that does not accept things at face value. This skepticism is crucial in creating an informed, active citizen who can say, "Wait a minute. That doesn't sound right to me," or "I want more information." Questioning cultivates the ability to interrogate the world on multiple levels and find information when needed.

Critical Thinking

Critical thinking is the ability to reason through a problem, take apart the components, and reassemble them in new ways. Critical thinking is the key to innovation. Students who can follow directions are a dime a dozen. To be engaged and active learners, students need to be able to interrogate a question or a problem and identify an outcome based on a series of reasons. This is a much more dynamic sense of engaging and using information instead of just learning it as flat content for future retrieval.

Hypothesizing

Hypothesizing is a key to understanding the world around us. We typically think of it in connection with science, but surmising about the cause of problems or events and then testing out ideas is central to all kinds of adult work and daily life as well as academic inquiry. "I didn't sleep well last night. Maybe it was because I drank that cup of coffee after dinner," is a hypothesis. In the next step, you might test it. What happens if you don't drink any coffee after dinner? This is how we learn: by trial and error. It's a simplified version of the scientific method.

Remember the image from the beginning of the chapter of the competent, thinking child with lots of ideas and theories about the world around them. This is a child who is hypothesizing. Reggio pedagogy supports children in hypothesizing. One way to value children's hypotheses is by asking children to express them. Here's an example.

At Pablo Neruda, on the occasion of each child's birthday there is a project each child participates in. This model is used in every class, but in different ways by different teachers in different groups. For instance, when a five-year-old turns six, Antonia asks them to identify a group of friends. On the birthday of the child in question, the friends selected meet in the mini-atelier and talk to Antonia about the birthday child. These conversations are then transcribed, and over the course of the year, they are put into a book featuring the children talking about each other. It is lovely and heartfelt.

When I was at Pablo Neruda, Paola and Patrizia shared with me a birthday project they had been working on with their four-year-old students. Paola and Patrizia would take the birthday child into the mini-atelier in their classroom and ask them, "Where do you think you were before you were born?" The responses would be recorded and transcribed. The children had real hypotheses and opinions about where they were before they were born. No one can say for sure where these ideas came from—stories they had been told or overheard, conversations, storybooks, or somewhere else. When Michele said he waited in the sky for his mama to call him, the teachers did not say no, that is impossible. They accepted these hypotheses. When I read through the notes and asked Paola about the project, she told me that the teachers' hypothesis was that perhaps the children did have some recollection of the time before they were born, since they were closer to the event than the adults. This is a great example of the teachers working out their hypotheses while the children shared their own.

Academics in the Emergent Classroom

Now let's take this general understanding of *intento progettuale* and look specifically at one academic skill that teachers are often concerned about in early childhood: reading. In Reggio, reading is not seen as a discrete competency the way that teachers and schools see it in the United States.

Reading is the ability to decode and understand symbols in increasingly more complex patterns. Children are reading long before they decode actual text. McDonald's golden arches, stop signs, traffic lights—our environment is full of recognizable symbols that children can read in much the same way that they will read their first sight words. This is the first kind of reading.

Sight words are the next step on the path of this symbol recognition. Children recognize words like "the," "and," "he," "she," "they," "Mom," "Dad," and their own names when they cannot sound these words out yet. As with the stop sign and the McDonald's arches, they do not need to sound these words out. They recognize them as symbols. The same is true of the first few hundred words that kids learn—they know them on sight. Children build up a sight word vocabulary largely as a result of being read to and flipping through pages studying the images and words they see as they listen to the story. Books for young children are largely comprised of sight words that children learn and recognize.

This foundation of words that children recognize on sight is the foundation that leads them to the next step: reading on their own. Reading is then the decoding of ever more complex combinations of sounds forming words and then words that form sentences, paragraphs, and stories.

Between the familiar sight words and the images that accompany the text in many books, children are able to tell or read the story using the symbolic cues (sight words, memory, and images) to construct the story. Think of the number of times you have been reading to children and tried to take shortcuts by editing the text down to wrap the story up more quickly. You've probably been corrected by an attentive listener, who tells you that no, that is not how the story goes, and you have missed something. Being able to tell the story from a combination of familiar sight words, memory, and illustrations is a genuine step in reading, not "pretend" reading or "prereading."

Children continue to increase the number of sight words they can recognize, while at the same time learning the sounds of the individual letters. They begin to sound out words they don't recognize until even those words become sight words. Most of the words that adults encounter when they read are sight words—adult readers recognize the word as a whole rather than laboriously sounding it out each time they see it. This is possible because adults have been reading for many years and have a large pool of sight words they have seen over and over again.

When I first started working at Pablo Neruda, I noticed that there were symbols on almost everything that also had a child's name on it. Children each had an individual symbol in addition to their name on their cubby, pillow, blanket—all of their personal things. At first I thought of this as "cute" but did not understand the learning embedded in this practice. In much of what happens in Reggio, there is a deeper meaning and intention that can escape even an experienced educator at first glance. When used with a group of children who spend three years together, these personal symbols contribute to the ability to recognize other symbols. The children come to know each other's symbols long before they are able to read each other's names. This clever use of symbols creates a scaffold that further supports the ability of children to acquire reading skills.

The symbols are a way of investing in the reading that children are *already* doing and strengthening their connection to and understanding of symbols in relationship to the world around them. The symbols support children's reading but not in the form of "readiness." They add to an environment that is designed for children in their current developmental stage *and* help develop what Americans might see as an academic skill.

The Shape of Things

Toward the end of my year in the four-year-old class with Paola and Patrizia I was able to witness a project that at first I did not understand. The class gathered found objects (shells, oranges, other fruit) from nature. Then they went about cutting the objects in half and examining the symmetry and shape. The students would draw or paint what they saw, drawing and painting being a couple of the ways offered to the children to explore the symmetrical objects. When it came time to put together the documentation panels, it started to become clear to me what the teachers were doing. They were exploring shapes in a completely different and deeper way than a typical American school might do. This exploration went beyond triangle, circle, and square to involve symmetry and the natural perfection and imperfections that can be found in the shapes of nature.

The exploration of what might otherwise be seen as academic concepts was thus naturally embedded into the daily life of the children. Paola and Patrizia knew that shapes and symmetry were timely topics. Children were involved in the selection and collection of objects, beginning with the way objects were gathered and then engaged. The shapes and their symmetry or lack thereof revealed themselves through the process of collection and examination accompanied by questions and dialogue. This is another example of intention in practice.

Segnalibro

Now let's take a look at one part of an intended project, *segnalibro*, or "bookmarker," that formed part of every child's experience when I was at Pablo Neruda. As part of this *intento progettuale* the teachers had identified their intention that students would both encounter and be drawn to books. This project began before the students even came to Pablo Neruda. The teachers met with the parents and talked to them about their children. In that conversation, they asked about the children's favorite books and how the students enjoyed or got close to books and characters.

As one part of *segnalibro,* a storytelling activity was conducted in an ongoing fashion, with a few children per week over the course of several months. Students brought their favorite books from home and read them to the class with varying degrees of accuracy and panache. The books were then made available in the classroom for the other students to enjoy, thus offering more opportunities for the students to engage with each other and the materials.

As part of the documentation, the teachers videotaped parts of these readings to share and discuss with parents. The recordings also joined the collection of artifacts as part of the documentation of the larger project. After each child read, the teachers would do a short one-on-one interview with the child that both demonstrated and pushed their metacognitive skills, enabling the students to talk about their process and reflect on their learning.

Here's how it went on one day. During the *assemblea*, Michele got up and took his book to the front of the class and read it. Then Paola and Patrizia interviewed him, asking him how he knew the story so well. He thought for a minute and said, "I hear my mama in my head." As Michele looked at the words and images on the pages, he was able to recall the story he had been read through the use of symbols and in collaboration with his own memory.

This is one example from one classroom with one group of students. The ideas might be adapted or exported, but the activities cannot be part of a checklist of things to do to enact the bookmarker project outside the schools of Reggio. This real-life example can spark ideas about what might work in your setting; it is not meant to persuade you to do exactly the same thing with your students. Instead, ask yourself: What is my intention for the children in my program?

One Reggio Program's Project Offerings

The schedule of projects on the next page is taken directly from my notes. It is organized according to categories I have created to make it easier to understand. This is just one week in one class at one school.

Be aware that this is merely a record of the projects that were offered at the end of the *assemblea* as children were split into groups. Some children may have participated in more than one of these, moving as their interests changed throughout the morning. Keep in mind that this is an example, not a model.

Sample Weekly Schedule from a Reggio Program

	Monday	Tuesday	Wednesday	Thursday	Friday
Environmental	Construction Houseplay Library Games Light table	Construction Houseplay Library Games Light table	Games Construction Houseplay Library Light table	Games Construction Houseplay Library Light table	Games Construction Houseplay Library
Emergent and Intended Projects	Atelier: *Colore tra le mani*	Segnalibro	Atelier: *Colore tra le mani*	Segnalibro	Atelier: *Colore tra le mani*
	Mini-atelier: Student-directed painting	Mini-atelier: Student–teacher discussion in small group	Mini-atelier: Student-directed painting	Mini-atelier: Student–teacher exploration of clay	Mini-atelier: Materials put out for student exploration (paper, pencils)
Self-Managed	Tabletop clouds	Tabletop clouds	Tabletop clouds	Tabletop clouds	Tabletop clouds

Notes

- The environmental projects are linked to areas in the classroom.
- This would be an example of what might be offered and the number of options children would be divided among.
- Some of these are self-directed, and others involve the teachers and the *atelierista*.

Reflect and Connect

After reading this chapter you may feel that what you know—what is literally the stuff of your memories and your education—has been flipped upside down. Try to look at these ideas as an extension of what you already know, instead of a replacement.

- Think about your own classroom. What skills and capabilities do you think are imperative for students to develop? These may be social-emotional, such as self-control or self-comfort, or relational, such as making friends or sharing, in addition to traditional academic skills.

- How might you create opportunities for these skills to be developed in your classroom? How might you create areas in the classroom to support those skills? For example, post offices, stores, and accounting firms can give students the setting to encounter skills and materials.

- Think back to chapter 4's discussion of *assemblea*. How might you extend discussions begun in your *assemblea* into the work times of your students?

- Finally, what are the things you think children will naturally explore? What do you already know children will encounter as they go through the year with you? What are the things they have a right to explore? Some possibilities are books, numeracy, themselves (their identity) and others, conflicts, friendships, and questions about why things are the way they are. What structures can you put in place to adequately capture and extend these moments when they arrive?

Learning and teaching should not stand on opposite banks and just watch the river flow by; instead, they should embark together on a journey down the water. Through an active, reciprocal exchange, teaching can strengthen learning how to learn.

—Loris Malaguzzi in *The Hundred Languages of Children*

Documentation as a Vehicle for Professional Development

This final chapter is a bit different from the five chapters that precede it, and more academic in tone. I include some of my recent research about documentation, which I believe to be a key to changing teacher practice. This chapter discusses the work I did for my dissertation, and as a result it is more complex than the other chapters. Citations in the text share the breadth and depth of thinking in the field about documentation. The references at the end of the book provide a list of all the sources I've cited in the chapter, in case you want to do some reading on your own. This is an opportunity for you to engage in rigorous, research-based reading that will inform your practice.

Teachers have experience and hunches about how and why things work with children. By engaging in deeper reflection and reading about topics you are interested in, you can compare your thinking with that of others and learn about what research can tell you about your field of work. This can affirm your hypotheses, push your thinking, and even help you revise your thoughts and actions.

Early childhood education can appear to occur in a vacuum, with teachers isolated in their rooms and programs isolated from one another. Ideally, teachers have colleagues to collaborate and compare their experiences with. In the absence of such opportunities, reading about others' experiences and ideas can help break down that isolation.

This chapter can help you better understand the broad reach of documentation within the context of professional development and the benefits of documentation beyond student learning, especially to teachers. The examination of literature here focuses exclusively on documentation, how it is used and linked to the schools of Reggio Emilia, and what other external influences may be germane to understanding how documentation works in early childhood and in Reggio-inspired programs.

I began my research with the hypothesis that through documentation, teachers can transform their own practice on a daily basis, changing professional development from something done on one or two days a year and outside of the classroom to something that is embedded in daily practice and linked to classroom work. I set about trying to test my hypothesis by doing an extensive literature review, which will be discussed in the next few pages. Then I asked teachers about their experience using documentation in their classrooms. I conducted an online survey with 606 educators. This chapter will use aspects of both the literature review and the research to explore the elements of documentation that I believe are critical to any journey into Reggio-inspired practice.

What Is Documentation?

Documentation is the process of making learning visible. This typically involves a number of concurrent and consecutive steps, the first of which is observation of the children and collection of artifacts. At the same time that they are observing and collecting, teachers are reflecting on and questioning what they are seeing, and talking to students about their work. Teachers are also hypothesizing about student growth and development. They use the collected artifacts and observations to fuel a cycle of inquiry around student learning based on what is seen and collected.

Documentation in Reggio Emilia

Documentation in Reggio Emilia has grown over fifty years to be one of the most important ways that teachers there understand and support children's learning.

Documentation makes student learning visible to teachers, other adults, and the students themselves, but perhaps more importantly it supports teachers in thinking deeply about children's learning and in putting the child at the center of the curriculum. In the Reggio schools and for those who follow this approach elsewhere, documentation has been identified as a pedagogical strategy that promotes collaboration, reflection, and meaning making among all members of the community, including children, parents, and teachers (Cadwell 2003; Goldhaber and Smith 2002).

The schools of Reggio take a whole new stance on the work students do and the way teachers engage with it. The approach challenges the traditional conceptions of a unidirectional teaching-learning relationship and instead argues that children and teachers are engaged in "a process of reciprocal learning" (Rinaldi 1998, 57). Throughout this process, children develop and test their theories about the world; alongside them, teachers engage in a similar process of discovery and inquiry, "leading to a deeper understanding of the children's meaning-making and correspondingly, to a rich and reflective pedagogy" (Goldhaber 2004, 76). This process of reciprocal learning gives teachers a chance to engage in professional development through the documentation of student work.

While in Reggio Emilia, I was able to work on my documentation practices alongside the teachers. This began with a focus on observing students and collecting information about them on my own and then, in collaboration with my colleagues, examining what I had written, reflecting on it, and pulling out threads of interest that the children demonstrated through their words or actions. I was like an apprentice: I received guidance, feedback, and support from the teachers I worked with. As I learned and my skills improved, I became increasingly interested in the possibilities that documentation offered to make teacher learning, as well as student learning, visible. I have continued to think about this potential while mentoring teachers who are working in a Reggio-inspired style in early childhood programs in the United States.

Documentation in the United States

Documentation is used spottily in American early childhood programs and often to support assessment and evaluation of children on a predetermined scale of growth and development.

A growing number of professionals are creating spaces within their classrooms for the use of documentation as a way of making student learning visible and accessible to others. American understanding of the role and benefits of documentation has traditionally focused exclusively on student learning. My work studied the process of documentation as a tool for teachers' professional development, building on the practices enacted in the Reggio Emilia preprimary schools (Edwards, Gandini, and Forman 1993; Wurm 2005).

Documentation and Teacher Transformation: A Literature Review

When you are studying a topic, one way to become informed is to see what has already been published about it. In academic circles, this is called a "literature review." It's like an online search in which you take the time to find out what already exists in the world about something you are interested in. For example, if you are looking to buy a new car, you may search for car reviews and manufacturer reports on the best models. If you did this kind of search, you would want to look at many sources, so you could get as much information as possible. Also, looking at many sources will help you identify disagreements or biases, as well as trends and omissions.

The same kind of process works in a literature review. It's an opportunity to take a look at what information already exists and what is being said and has been said over time about a specific topic. This enables you to take a broad look and can also illuminate how something has developed and what gaps exist. A literature review also helps to focus your research; it doesn't make sense to research a topic that has already been thoroughly explored.

My literature review focuses on documentation as a form of professional development, a way for teachers to inform and deepen their practice. I started the review as a way to find out what was already known about both documentation and teacher professional development. Within the literature review, the citations in parentheses after an idea tell you who has written or researched these ideas and the date of the publication about the topic. At the end of the book in the References section, you can look up the sources by name and year.

My research is concerned with early childhood practitioners, but this review of literature begins with broad definitions of professional development, which is a rich and well-researched topic in the literature. Looking at the broader picture helped me to identify and explore themes and gaps within professional development. After a general examination of professional development, I focused on specific aspects that lent themselves to my research. Seven key aspects of professional development emerged from my literature review:

- teacher learning and student learning
- teacher development
- problem setting
- communities of practice
- reflection
- teacher research
- documentation as a framework for teacher learning

Teacher Learning and Student Learning

Looking at students critically and with multiple lenses is not a new concept for American schools. However, the overlap between the ways students and teachers work and the idea that it can be a reciprocal process is still quite novel for many American educators (Carini and Himley 2000; Tyack 1974). In fact, the practices of documentation may be necessary to create reciprocal learning supported by the cycle of inquiry used by students and teachers—at times together, other times in parallel.

In opposition to the idea of "teacher training," Reggio Emilia educational models challenge the traditional conceptions of the teaching-learning relationship as being unidirectional and instead argue that children and teachers are engaged in "a process of reciprocal learning" (Rinaldi 1998, 121). Reggio-inspired practice establishes that knowledge building does not proceed in a linear, determined, and deterministic way or by progressive and predictable stages but rather is constructed through contemporaneous advances, may stand still, and may even backslide. This nonlinear view of learning, as a reciprocal process that involves teacher and student, situates inquiry as a fundamental way to ask and answer questions about the world.

This idea can also be found as a feature of "open education," which was introduced in the 1960s and '70s via the British infant schools and is grounded in principles of Piagetian theory (Inhelder and Piaget 1958). The role of inquiry within Reggio-inspired work is a tenet of the approach that unites both teacher and student, who build knowledge in similar ways. The conception of learning as something other than a unidirectional activity is not new to educational theory. Paulo Freire argued that teachers themselves have a difficult time getting past the "instilled certainty" (1973, 52) that teaching is lecturing and that knowledge is unidirectional. This process of multidirectional learning has been explored in research within schools and has been called "documentation as a cycle of inquiry" (Gandini and Goldhaber, 2001). I have engaged this concept as it informs teacher professional development, and my research shows that inquiry, enacted through documentation practices, serves many purposes in classrooms.

Teacher Development

Within the field of education, the learning that teachers do is called many things. Part of the challenge in conducting a review of literature on the subject of teacher professional development is exploring the diverse concepts within the literature. One theme I identified is that many ideas about professional development are fragmented and intellectually superficial and do not take into account what we know about how teachers learn (Ball and Cohen 1999; Borko 2004).

Traditional models of professional development have focused on expanding the individual repertoire of well-defined classroom practices and developing curricular materials. These more traditional approaches follow a lecture or workshop model with topics selected by those who are not working in classrooms. They present content and strategies that may be valuable but are disconnected from the daily life of schools and teachers and therefore gain little traction in practice. Some writers believe that the traditional approaches to professional development, which have been dominated by a training and coaching model, do not stand up to the emerging needs of teachers (Little 1993).

It has become popular in recent years to focus teacher professional development on action research, teacher research, reflective practice, and collaborative inquiry processes (Kraft 2002). Emerging approaches involving collaboration, assessment, and inquiry demonstrate the recognition that professional development can be rooted in classroom practice (Borko 2004, 10; Little 1993, 136). Models that are linked to classrooms and individual teacher practice, like action research, have gained in popularity and also enable teachers to use their own challenges as learning opportunities.

Problem Setting

Professional practice has been called a process of problem solving (Schön 1983). Problems of choice or decision making are solved through the selection, from available means, of the one solution best suited to established ends. But with this emphasis on problem solving, we ignore problem setting, the process by which the teacher defines the decision to be made, the ends to be achieved, the means that may be chosen. In real-world practice, problems do not present themselves to the practitioner as givens. They must be constructed from the materials of problem situations that are puzzling, troubling, and uncertain (Schön 1987, 40). This is a key problem of more traditional professional development opportunities: problems are being solved divorced from classroom practice. Teachers should be involved in the problem setting as well.

This reinforces that traditional models that have consisted of "short-term or one-shot in-service programs conducted by outside experts" are not effective at fostering teacher development (Cullen 1997, 21). What has also become evident through this part of the review of literature is that "both educators and researchers attempted to alter methods of teacher professional development so that teachers assume control of classroom decisions and actively participate in their own instructional improvement on an on-going basis" (Hopkins 1985, 78). Ultimately, how adults approach their own learning provides a model for children's emerging views of learning (Meagher 2006).

Communities of Practice

Communities of practice, which can also be called "professional learning communities" or "reflective practice groups," have been identified throughout the literature as constructs that contribute to teacher development. They have been explored as ways to ease new teachers into their jobs, but I also looked at the research on communities of practice designed for teachers' ongoing professional development. As Judy Harris Helm explains, "early educators can recognize communities of practice as a legitimate approach to professional development" (2007, 15).

Wenger (1998) describes communities of practice as an informal approach to professional development characterized by collaborative mutual engagement, in which the emphasis on learning is through social interaction. It seems clear from his work that communities of practice can fuel individual teachers' attention to their practice and can provide a powerful research instrument for learning with the collaboration of colleagues. Involvement in communities of practice can vary at different stages of a teacher's career (pre-service, induction, ongoing professional development), and the experience has been examined in each of these unique stages along the teacher career timeline (Borko and Putnam 1996; Wenger 2000a).

My research on communities of practice brought to mind Lev Vygotsky's notions of the power of socially constructed learning (Vermette, Harper, and DiMillo 2004): there is real power in collaborative and cooperative learning for both students and teachers. Further, Wenger notes that communities of practice manage to cultivate organizational forms without too tightly mandating participation. Wenger defines these communities of practice as "groups of people who share a concern or passion for something they do and learn how to do it better through interacting with one another" (2000b, 141). It has been found that effective communities of practice share some common hallmarks: they focus on solutions, cultivate best practices, and develop professional skills. A compilation of a number of other sources on communities of practice has put forth six attributes that contribute to a successful community of practice for educators:

- shared belief/vision
- strong leadership
- shared practice
- organizational supports
- collaboration and application
- time/resource dedication

Communities of practice foster both collaboration and reflection, and it is here that problem solving related to students and collective inquiry affect ongoing professional development at school sites (DuFour, DuFour, Eaker, and Karhanek 2004; Hord and Sommers 2008).

While communities of practice offer opportunities to both collaborate and reflect, researchers acknowledge that these are not easy skills to cultivate (Meagher 2006). But it's clear that the collaboration fostered through communities of practice yields positive benefits for participants. "A culture of collaboration and a focus upon instruction is transformational: it infuses the institution, impacting productivity, morale, teacher retention, public perception and, ultimately, student achievement" (Bloom and Stein 2004, 21). Collaboration is not always reflected in organized offerings of professional development, although most professionals agree that it is a worthy goal (Walther-Thomas, Korinek, and McLaughlin 1999). According to Walther-Thomas and colleagues, effective collaboration emerges out of concerns by individuals who are like-minded and care deeply about the same issues. Some guidelines for effective collaboration have been established, including these four:

- Friendship is not a prerequisite.
- Time is necessary to build trust and enable teams to work well together.
- Participation is voluntary.
- Guidelines for decision making should be established.

The literature indicates that when professional development takes place within schools, there is a stronger collaborative experience. Day writes that "collaborative forms of inquiry deeply embedded in the context and ways of working of schools may offer transformational and enhancing opportunities for professional development" (2004, 122). Collaboration is also frequently cited as contributing significantly to well-being and productivity in schools (Darling-Hammond 1998; Slavin 1995).

Through my experience in the schools of Reggio Emilia, I have seen the important and vital ways that collaboration can manifest and contribute to the dialogue and inquiry in process. Collaboration leads to lasting improvements in teaching (Meagher 2006).

Project Zero, hosted at Harvard University, has conducted research within the schools of Reggio Emilia in an effort to understand documentation and promote learning groups in schools (2001). The project is building on previous research to help create communities of reflective, independent learners; to enhance understanding within and across disciplines; and to promote critical and creative thinking. Visible Thinking, a program of Project Zero, is an approach to teaching and learning that emphasizes the use of thinking routines and documentation to make thinking more visible in classrooms. Visible Thinking was included in the research and collaboration done within the schools of Reggio Emilia (Cox 2006; Donovan and Sutter 2004).

Reflection

In addition to the work that takes place in relation to collaboration within communities of practice, the literature also identifies reflection as crucial to the development of teachers and supported in these communities. Reflection is defined as an intellectual strategy to look at and improve teacher practice (Bennett 2007; Dewey [1933] 1960). The basic reflective processes, through collaboration with others, becomes a true conversation of practice (Yinger 1990). Or, in the words of Dewey, "if we are going to be more effective teachers we need to become more reflective teachers. To be more reflective we need to articulate our theories of learning, critically examine them and replace those parts which we suspect, or better still can show, do not work" ([1933] 1960, 54). The goal for professional development has been identified as creating a full network of collaborative options that teachers can use to support the development of their reflective practices (Yinger 1990).

Schön (1983) adds to the conversation by telling us that when a practitioner reflects in and on her practice, the possible objects of her reflection are as varied as the kinds of phenomena before her and the systems of knowing-in-practice that she brings to them. She may reflect on the tacit norms that underlie a judgment or on the strategies and theories implicit in a pattern of behavior. She may reflect on the feeling for a situation that has led her to adopt a particular course of action, on the way in which she has framed the problem she is trying to solve, or on the role she has constructed for herself within a larger institutional context (62).

Teacher Research

Marilyn Cochran-Smith (2005) suggests that the teacher's task is to function simultaneously as both researcher and practitioner. Cochran-Smith and Lytle define teacher research as "systematic and intentional inquiry about teaching, learning, and schooling carried out by teachers in their own school and classroom settings" (1993, 27). Tension exists between conceptions of teacher research and documentation, although they also overlap.

Teacher research as professional development has been found to have a profound effect on those who have performed it (Atay 2008, 140). And increasing numbers of teachers are conducting research in their own classrooms and schools in cooperation with their colleagues (Corcoran 1995, 3). It is especially useful for teachers to be focusing this research on problems identified by teachers themselves (4). Additionally, embedding professional development in the workplace so it is closely related to teachers' work experience encourages discussion, reflection, and collaboration, all key components of successful professional development (4).

Although there is growing literature on the positive outcomes associated with teachers doing research, not much information is available about the specific characteristics and stages of the research process. It is here that the components of documentation in the schools of Reggio Emilia provide a framework for examining the process and benefits more closely (Atay 2008, 140).

Documentation as a Framework for Teacher Learning

Embedded all the way through the process of documentation are reflection, collaboration, motivation, and the commitment of time. Teacher research includes teacher questions as a key element to driving the research process, and teacher questions are also used to shape documentation practices. In my experience projects beginning from questions that emerge in classrooms can be positioned to lead the documentation process that includes these four elements measured in this study; alternately, documentation can simply be a process of revealing patterns that are embedded within student activity in the classroom and then lead to formalized questions on the part of the teachers. In this way the documentation can emerge from questions or vice versa.

Documentation as a component of the cycle of inquiry has been understood as a way to make learning visible (Rinaldi 1998). It is through this process of documentation that shifts in thinking can be observed. "Transformative learning has been understood as effective at capturing the meaning-making process of adult learners, particularly the learning process" (Taylor 2008, 174).

Documentation has also been used as a framework for action research. For example, a teacher discusses her experience documenting student work: "I've been able to see power. . . . This effort produces a space for thinking about teaching, which can change the way you look at classrooms and enlarge the way you imagine school" (Carini and Himley 2000, 58). Carini and Himley followed a group of teachers who have established a learning collaborative in which they look at students and their development from unique perspectives and within a structure that aligns very well with the literature already reviewed in this chapter. The process of documentation is highly structured, a characteristic that is identified as important for the success of communities of practice and useful in promoting teacher collaboration and reflection—key aspects of meaningful professional engagement. Not only are reflection and collaboration powerful tools toward teacher refinement, but they are largely controlled by teachers themselves.

The media coverage of the schools of Reggio Emilia and evolving links between teacher inquiry and documentation practices has helped to make American ideas of teacher development more tightly connected to reflection and other aspects of adult learning (Atay 2008; Cheyney 2008; Cochran-Smith 2005; Mezirow 1991). As teachers examine children's work and prepare the documentation of it, their own understanding of children's development and insight into their learning are deepened in ways not likely to occur from inspecting test results.

Documentation provides a basis for the modification and adjustment of teaching strategies, and a source of ideas for new strategies, while deepening the teacher's awareness of each child's progress. The rich data made available through documentation can include (but are not limited to) strategies children use to engage each other, strategies children use to engage materials, norms that are established within classes surrounding arrival and departure, the development of concepts of print, and engagement with literature, color, or tools. By examining the documented steps taken by children during their investigations and representational work, the teacher can gain knowledge of each child's unique construction of their experience and the ways group efforts contribute to their learning (Katz and Chard 1996).

Making learning visible is of particular relevance to American educators. Documentation provides information about children's learning and progress that cannot be demonstrated by the formal standardized tests and checklists they commonly employ. While US teachers often gain important information and insight from their own firsthand observations of children, documentation of the children's work provides compelling evidence of the intellectual powers of young children while engaging the teachers as learners in the process.

My Research on Documentation

My literature review showed that teacher development is critical to student success. The study I conducted focused on common activities in early childhood settings. I looked at the effects documentation had on the development of teachers as they engaged in it as part of their daily work. To do so, I identified four factors that are critical to both documentation and professional development: motivation, time, reflection, and collaboration.

Documentation, in the forms of observation of children and extensive record keeping, has long been encouraged and practiced in many early childhood programs (Almy and Genishi 1979; Cohen et al. 1997; Katz and Chard 1996). Documentation in Reggio Emilia focuses intensively on children's experiences, memories, thoughts, and ideas in the course of their work. Collection and analysis of artifacts reveals patterns and supports hypotheses for and about the learner. This includes teachers' written observations, audio and video recordings, photographs, and children's two- and three-dimensional artifacts that render learning visible and accessible to interpretation and reflection.

Documentation practices in Reggio Emilia provide inspiring examples of the importance of displaying children's work with great care and attention to both the content and the aesthetic aspects of the display. To best discuss these practices I have listed some terms below and explained how they are used in this chapter and my research.

- Professional development: Teachers' ongoing learning about their professional practice once they have completed their in-service training and have taken a position in a school.
- Collaboration: The activity of working in groups as they are conceived within schools and across subject matter in loosely defined and self-directed ways. Collaboration is recognized as a way to foster knowledge sharing and skill development.
- Reflection: Critical self-examination as related to process, action, and thought. Reflection is defined as an intellectual strategy to look at and improve teacher practice (Bennett 2007; Dewey [1933] 1960; Schön 1987).
- Motivation: The force that moves an individual or group to action, which may originate internally or externally.
- Time: The resources allocated as measured in minutes, hours, days, weeks, months, and years. The availability or lack of time is also a component of the way time is understood for this study.

Documentation linked to the cycle of inquiry is at the heart of working in Reggio-inspired ways. It is based on questions and the inquirers' ability to engage in the process of hypothesizing, gathering artifacts, and reflecting that leads to insights, ideas, and confirmation or nullification of the original hypothesis.

The process of documentation requires reflecting on a number of things. To begin with, the teacher looks at the artifacts collected and reflects on them to identify patterns across and between types of artifacts. Patterns fall into categories like these:

- language
- behavior
- problem-solving strategies
- social strategies, groupings, or leadership

- approaches to one another
- approaches to meeting the materials
- response
- emotions

The teacher may also reflect on the interactions between themselves and the students, or among the students, or between the students and the materials or environment. The possibilities within these broad categories are almost endless.

The Survey

This research was conducted using an online survey that analyzed and aggregated responses of more than six hundred early childhood educators. The survey was developed through the use of one qualitative study and one pilot study, with much discussion and reflection between each iteration. The pilot survey consisted of eighteen questions designed to focus on the overlap that exists between conceptions of documentation and conceptions of transformative learning. The final survey consisted of a total of thirty questions, of which seven were qualitative and not used in the data analyses. The survey also included eight demographic questions. A copy of the survey and some of the results are in the appendix.

The participants in the survey were solicited from a number of sources in an effort to get a broad representation of professionals in the field. The development of the survey began in January 2009; the first survey was administered to forty-four teachers in order to develop the language to best describe and discuss their practice. This was a qualitative instrument consisting of a series of open-ended questions and was posted on a Listserv of those early childhood educators who elected to respond.

The responses were divided for analysis in two ways: by individual participant and by question.

What the Research Measured

I asked teachers about the work they were doing and the value and time they put into it as an attempt to measure whether documentation was a transformative process for them. My research was framed by three overarching questions:

1. Do teachers report that there are benefits to their practice as a result of documenting student work?
2. For those who report benefits, what benefits to their work are reported as a result of documentation?
3. Can benefits to teacher development be inferred from the documentation practices as reported by teachers?

In sorting the survey responses, I sought to examine patterns that existed between the four concepts defined above: collaboration, reflection, motivation, and time. When I analyzed the data gathered through the survey, I looked at each of the individual concepts as well as the relationship between them.

Out of the 606 teachers who participated in the survey, 575 said that they engage in documentation practices in their classrooms. This was a welcome finding to set the tone for the data analysis. Of those 575 respondents, 409 indicated they believed engagement in documentation benefits teachers.

There were a number of unexpected results. Never having done a study of this size or type, I was unsure of how the data would reveal themselves, and only through doing many variations of the analyses was I able to see patterns across the responses that were not visible at first.

The most surprising and initially clear finding was the high level of reported engagement in documentation and the value educators place on the practice of documentation. Although I had hypothesized that documentation benefits teachers' practices, I did not anticipate such a clear recognition by early childhood educators of the high value of documentation to their own practice. This value is, of course, beyond the benefits to students and families. The fact that over 70 percent of those who responded say there are benefits to teachers was a surprising result.

Here are some other results of the research:

- There is evidence of strong links between time and motivation; they are difficult to separate, as one is indicative of another.
- The responses clearly indicated the importance of both of these factors (time and motivation) as well as the presence of motivation

on the part of respondents to do more, do better, and dedicate more time to documentation as part of their professional practice.

- Additionally, a link between reflection and collaboration emerged. This had been identified in the review of literature but emerged strongly as part of the respondents' experience with documentation.
- The findings of collaboration and reflection, while present, linked, and measurable, were overshadowed by the links between time and motivation.
- One of the strongest themes was related to the time educators reported they spend on documentation and the motivation they have to spend more time doing these activities.
- According to the analysis, the lowest reported response on documentation was about the respondents' ability to collaborate with colleagues (self-reported at 32 percent). This was a significantly low number, especially in light of all the literature focused on the importance of collaboration as part of professional development.

Research Takeaways for Teachers

What do these results mean for you as you work to strengthen your documentation? I will summarize the most important insights. (If you are interested in the original project analysis, see the appendix.) In doing this research I wanted to see if documentation, as it happens every day in classrooms, could transform teacher practice. I believe that by doing documentation daily, teachers would have ample opportunities to develop their skills. Supporting the potential for teacher development inside the classroom is an easier and more efficient approach to teacher education than working on development divorced from classroom practice. The literature review helped me identify what aspects of professional development and teacher transformation and documentation were the most important to measure. The survey helped me measure the four factors of motivation, time, collaboration, and reflection, which tie documentation, professional development, and teacher transformation together.

Motivation

Fundamental to documentation is having motivation. No one can do documentation for you, and yet as a teacher you are commonly time-strapped. In order to document what is happening with the children in your classroom, you have to decide you want to do it, even if just for ten minutes a day. Ten minutes a day is fifty minutes a week and two hundred minutes a month—more than three hours! Teachers expressed great motivation but felt there were roadblocks to their desire. I do not have the answers to get around all of them, but I know that motivation is the key to finding a way.

Time

The next vital component is the time to engage. Sneaking a few minutes here and there—eating lunch with the teachers in the room next to you so you can talk about documentation or working in the art studio while children nap—still has value. When we think about time, it is typically in large blocks, but a little bit can take you a long way, whether it's in collecting artifacts, observing children, collaborating with colleagues, or keeping a reflection journal.

Also, my research found a tight connection between time and motivation. The research doesn't necessarily show causation, but it does show a correlation between the two factors. One way to interpret this might be that if you make the time for documentation, you feel more motivated. Another way to look at it: the more motivated you are, the easier it is to find the time. Either way, it's clear that the two work together: when one increases, the other follows suit.

Collaborating with Colleagues

My research showed the teachers are not comfortable collaborating with other teachers despite all of the evidence that points to it as a powerful habit. Collaborating at school sites can have many challenges—time in general, time without kids, the lack of protocol that keeps people on task, and the lack of structures that make everyone feel safe enough to share. There is plenty written about how to manage these challenges. The bottom line is that you do not have to collaborate with your colleagues to document what's happening with your children, but if you want to become a better teacher, it's critical to find a way through your discomfort. Collaboration is central to documentation in the Reggio schools, and it's hard to imagine the schools being as powerful for children, or as shining an example to American education as they are, without it. There will always be a reason why you cannot do it. You just have to make the time and find a way.

According to my research, teachers are more comfortable collaborating with parents and students than with their colleagues. At the same time, what kind of collaboration will push your practice to the next level? My literature review is clear: collaborating with colleagues makes an enormous difference in teachers' development over time. This is borne out by the experience of teachers in Reggio Emilia; they teach and document children's work and learning in collaborative teams. This means that to improve, teachers need to share and receive feedback on their own work; they can benefit from opening up the doors to their classrooms and their practice to one another and from working together in the spirit of authentic growth.

The research also indicated that teachers improved other important skills of documentation by collaborating with each other. These skills included the following:

- collecting work of students
- conducting observations
- listening to children
- note taking
- reflecting with students and colleagues
- sharing with children

You can see that collaborating brings more than the obvious benefits.

Also worth noting is another type of collaboration that teachers identified as important: the support of the school administration.

Reflection

Reflection is a key competency to refining your practice. The literature and my research showed that reflection helped teachers see how their work fits into a larger context.

My research found that documentation influenced teacher practice. Teachers said that documentation

- makes me more reflective
- helps me slow down
- supports collaboration with my colleagues
- gets me to look at the children more carefully.

These results lead to transforming teacher practice.

Reflect and Connect

- How do these research findings relate to your own experience with documentation and your development as a teacher?
- What might you do this week to collaborate more with your colleagues?
- Are you reflecting verbally or in a journal each day? This is documentation. How can you make this part of your everyday practice?

Research Survey

The Final Survey Used
for Data Collection

1. Do you use documentation in your classroom?
    ☐ Yes   ☐ No

2. How would you define documentation? (Please select all that apply).
    ☐ Telling a story
    ☐ Physical representation of work
    ☐ Process to make learning visible
    ☐ Collection of information used to assess and plan
    ☐ Recording children's work and ideas and making these visible
    for parents, children and teachers
    ☐ Compiling children's work to show the experiences that occur

3. Other (please specify)
    _____
    _____

4. Which of the following would you identify as components
    of the documentation process?
    ☐ evaluating student work
    ☐ display of final product
    ☐ sharing with children
    ☐ reflecting on process with colleagues
    ☐ reflecting with children
    ☐ sorting artifacts
    ☐ re-visiting work in process
    ☐ collecting work of students
    ☐ photographing
    ☐ recording conversations
    ☐ conducting observations
    ☐ getting feedback from colleagues/parents
    ☐ note taking
    ☐ transcribing recorded conversations
    ☐ listening to children

5. Other (please specify)

   _____

   _____

6. Using the components of documentation selected in question 4, please share how often you do these activities.

QUALIFIERS

	Monthly	Every couple of weeks	Weekly	Daily
evaluating student work				
display of final product				
sharing with children				
reflecting on process with colleagues				
reflecting with children				
sorting artifacts				
re-visiting work in process				
collecting work of students				
photographing				
recording conversations				
conducting observations				
getting feedback from colleagues/parents				
note taking				
transcribing recorded conversations				
listening to children				

7. Please indicate which of these activities you think you would benefit with more time to do.

QUALIFIERS

	Enough time spent now	Would like more time	I need to spend less time	N/A
collecting work of students				
conducting observations				
display of final product				
evaluating student work				
hypothesizing				
listening to children				
note taking				
photographing				
recording conversations				
reflecting on process with colleagues				
reflecting with children				
re-visiting work in process				
sharing with children				
sorting artifacts				
transcribing recorded conversations				

8. In what ways could your practice benefit from more time on the above activities?

_____

_____

9. Would you say there are benefits for teachers
    in documenting student work?
    ☐ Yes   ☐ No

10. What would you say these benefits are for the teacher?
    ☐ Communication
    ☐ Teacher thinking
    ☐ Parent participation
    ☐ Skill acquisition
    ☐ Classroom process
    ☐ Insight into child's learning

11. Are there any benefits to teachers that you think should be
    added to this list?

    _____

    _____

12. Please choose any of the following activities that you would report as
    beneficial to your own practice as a professional (as you encounter them
    while documenting student work).
    ☐ listening to children
    ☐ sorting artifacts
    ☐ display of final product
    ☐ hypothesizing
    ☐ photographing
    ☐ note taking
    ☐ recording conversations
    ☐ evaluating student work
    ☐ conducting observations
    ☐ re-visiting work in process
    ☐ sharing with children
    ☐ reflecting on process with colleagues
    ☐ transcribing recorded conversations
    ☐ reflecting with children

13. How have these activities been beneficial to you as a teacher?

QUALIFIERS

	Has deepened my under-standing of children	Has made me more reflective	Has enabled me to collabo-rate with my colleagues	Has contrib-uted to the culture of my school
listening to children				
sorting artifacts				
display of final product				
hypothesizing				
photographing				
note taking				
recording conversations				
evaluating student work				
conducting observations				
re-visiting work in process				
sharing with children				
reflecting on process with colleagues				
transcribing recorded conversations				
reflecting with children				

14. Are there barriers to engaging in the work of documentation in your present setting?
☐ Yes ☐ No

15. If yes, what are these barriers?

   _____

   _____

   _____

16. Are there particular factors that support the process of documentation
   at your present setting?
      ☐ Yes   ☐ No

17. Which of these factors support the process of documentation
   in your present setting?
      ☐ Release time
      ☐ Collaboration with colleagues
      ☐ Support from administration
      ☐ Time outside of school
      ☐ Planning to get it done
      ☐ Experience with documentation

18. Are there things you can think of to share that would motivate you
   in your process of documentation?

   _____

   _____

   _____

19. As part of the documentation process, do you collect your own
   work samples?
      ☐ Yes   ☐ No

20. How would you say collecting your own work samples
   influences your practice?
      ☐ Makes me more reflective
      ☐ Helps me slow down
      ☐ Supports collaboration with my colleagues
      ☐ Gets me to look at the children more carefully

21. Which of the activities described in the previous question do you think are most important to your growth as a teacher?

	True	Not true	Not sure
Makes me more reflective			
Helps me slow down			
Supports collaboration with my colleagues			
Gets me to look at the children more carefully			

22. Is there anything that you would like to share about your documentation experiences or practices that you feel is important and has not been touched upon?

_____

_____

_____

_____

_____

Please include the following demographic information:

23. Age _____

24. Gender _____

25. Education level _____

26. Years in field _____

27. Current role _____

28. Past role _____

29. State _____

30. Continent _____

Survey Results

I was able to isolate the four operating concepts as identified and explore them in the bivariate and multivariate analysis. For the analysis related directly to the research questions, some additional configurations were created. The research questions of the study were:

1. Do teachers report that there are benefits to their practice as a result of documenting student work?
2. For those who report benefits, what benefits to their work are reported as a result of the documentation process?
3. What overlap exists between teacher-reported benefits to their own practice and aspects of Mezirow's transformative theory as adapted by Fetherston and Kelly (2007)?
4. Can benefits to teacher development be inferred from the documentation practices as reported by teachers?

1. Do teachers report that there are benefits to their practice as a result of documenting student work?

Benefits to Teachers Who Document Student Work

Questions	# Who Answered Yes
Do you use documentation in your classroom?	575
Would you say there are benefits for teachers in documentation?	439

By doing a multivariate analysis of those who reported they do document with the responses to "Would you say there are benefits?" there is an affirmative response of 76 percent of responses.

2. For those who report benefits, what benefits to their work are reported as a result of the documentation process?

Benefits to Teacher Thinking as a Result of Documenting Student Work

Questions	# Who Answered Yes
Do you use documentation in your classroom?	575
Would you say there are benefits to teachers in documentation?	439
What would you say these benefits are to teachers? Teacher thinking	351

Benefits to Parent Participation as a Result of Documenting Student Work

Questions	# Who Answered Yes
Do you use documentation in your classroom?	575
Would you say there are benefits to teachers in documentation?	439
What would you say these benefits are to teachers? Parent participation	298

Benefits to Overall Communication as a Result of Documenting Student Work

Questions	# Who Answered Yes
Do you use documentation in your classroom?	575
Would you say there are benefits to teachers in documentation?	439
What would you say these benefits are to teachers? Communication	336

To examine the specific benefits as they are aligned with this study, I conducted a multivariate analysis, layering those who document with those who believe there are benefits to teachers, and then I selected each of the benefits as the third component of the analysis.

Aggregated Benefits to Documenting Student Work

Teacher thinking	Parent participation	Communication
351 or 61%	298 or 52%	336 or 58%

3. What overlap exists between teacher-reported benefits to their own practice and aspects of Mezirow's transformative theory as adapted by Featherston and Kelly (2007)?

I isolated the framing components of the study: reflection, collaboration, time, and motivation. Within each category, I placed the percentage of educators who answered affirmatively.

Reflection

The number of educators who indicated reflection was a part of their process was over half across analyses.

Aggregated Benefits to Reflection as a Result of Documenting Student Work

With colleagues	With students	With parents
53.4%	60%	56%

Collaboration

The number of educators who indicated that collaboration was a part of their documentation practice was split along interesting lines—with colleagues the number was low, but with students and parents it rose to between one-half and two-thirds.

Aggregated Influence on Collaboration as a Result of Documenting Student Work

With colleagues	With students	With parents
32.5%	60%	56%

Time and Motivation

Both time and motivation were clearly represented as aspects of the documentation practices of the educators who engaged the study.

Desire to Spend More Time on Aspects of Documentation

Daily	Weekly	Monthly
73%	68.5%	66.2%

Motivation to Spend More Time
as Linked to Seen Benefits
from Documenting Student Work

Daily	Weekly	Monthly
73%	67.1%	69.7%

4. Can benefits to teacher development be inferred from the documentation practices as reported by teachers?

Yes, 439 out of 575 (or 76.3 percent) of respondents who documented affirmed the benefits to their practice.

References

Chapter 1

Chomsky, N. (1965). *Aspects of the theory of syntax*. MIT Press.
Spelke, E. S., and K. D. Kinzler. (2007). Core knowledge. *Developmental Science* 10 (1): 89–96.

Chapter 3

Deal, T. E., and K. D. Peterson. (1999). *Shaping school culture: The heart of leadership*. San Francisco: Jossey-Bass.
Elias, M. J., J. E. Zins, R. P. Weissberg, K. S. Frey, M. T. Greenberg, N. M. Haynes, et al. (1997). *Promoting social and emotional learning: Guidelines for educators*. Alexandria, VA: Association for Supervision and Curriculum Development.
Zins, J. E., M. R. Bloodworth, R. P. Weissberg, and H. J. Walberg. (2004). The scientific base linking emotional learning to student success and academic outcomes. In *Building academic success on social and emotional learning: What does the research say?*, ed. J. E. Zins, R. P. Weissberg, M. C. Wang, and H. J. Walberg, 3–22. New York: Teachers College Press.

Chapter 6

Almy, M., and C. Genishi. (1979). *Ways of studying children*. Rev. ed. New York: Teachers College Press.
Atay, D. (2008). Teacher research for professional development. *ELT Journal* 62 (2): 139–47.

Ball, D. L., and D. K. Cohen. (1999). Developing practice, developing practitioners: Toward a practice-based theory of professional education. In *Teaching as the learning profession: Handbook of policy and practice*, ed. L. Darling-Hammond and G. Sykes. San Francisco: Jossey-Bass.

Bennett, T. (2007). New ways of preparing high-quality teachers. *Young Children* 62 (4): 32–33.

Bloom, G., and R. Stein. (2004). Building practice. *Leadership* 34 (1): 20–22.

Borko, H. (2004). Professional development and teacher learning: Mapping the terrain. *Educational Researcher* 33 (8): 3–15.

Borko, H., and R. T. Putnam. (1996). Learning to teach. In *Handbook of educational psychology*, ed. D. C. Berliner and R. C. Calfee, 673–709. New York: Macmillan.

Cadwell, L. B. (2003). *Bringing learning to life: A Reggio approach to early childhood education.* New York: Teachers College Press.

Carini, P. F., and M. Himley. (2000). *From another angle: Children's strengths and school standards: The Prospect Center's descriptive review of the child.* Practitioner Inquiry. New York: Teachers College Press.

Cheyney, K. (2008). Collaborative learning communities: The power of teacher research and collaboration. *Exchange: The Early Childhood Leaders Magazine* 180: 10–13.

Cochran-Smith, M. (2005). *Policy, practice and politics in teacher education: Editorials for the Journal of Teacher Education.* Thousand Oaks, CA: Corwin Press, Sage, and American Association of Colleges for Teacher Education.

Cochran-Smith, M., and S. L. Lytle. (1993). *Inside out: Teacher research and knowledge.* New York: Teachers College Press.

Cohen, D. H., V. Stern, and N. Balaban. (1997). *Observing and recording the behavior of young children.* New York: Teachers College Press.

Corcoran, T. (1995). Helping teachers teach well: Transforming professional development. *CPRE Policy Briefs*, 1–7.

Cox Suárez, S. (2006). Making learning visible through documentation: Creating a culture of inquiry among pre-service teachers. *New Educator* 2 (1): 33–55.

Cullen, R. (1997). Transfer of training assessing the impact of INSET in Tanzania. In *In-service teacher development: International perspectives*, ed. D. Hayes. London: Prentice-Hall.

Darling-Hammond, L. (1998). Teacher learning that supports student learning. *Educational Leadership* 55 (5): 6–11.

Day, C. (2004). *A passion for teaching*. London: RoutledgeFalmer.

Dewey, J. (1933/1960). *How we think*. Lexington, MA: Heath.

Donovan, M., and C. Sutter. (2004). Encouraging doubt and dialogue: Documentation as a tool for critique. *Language Arts* 81 (5): 377–84.

DuFour, R., R. DuFour, R. Eaker, and G. Karhanek. (2004). *Whatever it takes: How a professional learning community responds when kids don't learn*. Bloomington, IN: Solution Tree (formerly National Educational Service).

Edwards, C., L. Gandini, and G. Forman, eds. (1993). *The hundred languages of children: The Reggio Emilia approach to early childhood education*. Norwood, NJ: Ablex.

Freire, P. (1973). *Education for critical consciousness*. New York: Seabury Press.

Gandini, L., and J. Goldhaber. (2001). Two reflections about documentation. In *Bambini: The Italian approach to infant/toddler care*, ed. L. Gandini and C. Pope Edwards. New York: Teachers College Press.

Goldhaber, J. (2004). The development of an early childhood teacher research collaborative. *Theory into Practice* 46 (1): 74–80.

Goldhaber, J., and V. R. Smith. (2002). The development of documentation strategies to support teacher reflection, inquiry, and collaboration. In *Teaching and learning: Collaborative exploration of the Reggio Emilia approach*, ed. V. R. Fu, A. J. Stremmel, and L. T. Hill, 147–60. Upper Saddle River, NJ: Merrill Prentice Hall.

Helm, J. H. (2007). Energizing your professional development by connecting with a purpose: Building communities of practice. *Young Children* 62 (4): 12–17.

Hopkins, D. (1985). *A teacher's guide to classroom research*. Philadelphia: Open University Press.

Hord, S. M., and M. A. Sommers. (2008). *Leading professional learning communities: Voices from research and practice*. Thousand Oaks, CA: Corwin Press.

Inhelder, B., and J. Piaget. (1958). *The growth of logical thinking from childhood to adolescence*. New York: Basic Books.

Katz, L. G., and S. C. Chard. (1996). The contribution of documentation to the quality of early childhood education. *ERIC Digest*.

Kraft, N. P. (2002). Teacher research as a way to engage in critical reflection: A case study. *Reflective Practice* 3 (2): 175–89.

Little, J. W. (1993). Teachers' professional development in a climate of educational reform. *Educational Evaluation and Policy Analysis* 15 (2): 129–51.

Meagher, S. (2006). Don't hesitate: Collaborate. *Teaching Pre K-8* 36 (6): 66–67.

Mezirow, J. (1991). *Transformative dimensions of adult learning.* San Francisco: Jossey-Bass.

Project Zero and Reggio Children. (2001). *Making learning visible: Children as individual and group learners.* Reggio Emilia, Italy: Reggio Children.

Rinaldi, C. (1998). Projected curriculum constructed through documentation: *Progettazione.* In *The hundred languages of children: The Reggio Emilia approach—Advanced reflections,* ed. C. Edwards, L. Gandini, and G. Forman, 113–25. 2nd ed. Norwood, NJ: Ablex.

Schön, D. A. (1983). *The reflective practitioner: How professionals think in action.* New York: Basic Books.

Schön, D. A. (1987). *Educating the reflective practitioner.* San Francisco: Jossey-Bass.

Slavin, R. E. (1995). *Cooperative learning: Theory, research, and practice.* 2nd ed. Boston: Allyn & Bacon.

Taylor, E. W. (2008). Transformative learning theory. *New Directions for Adult and Continuing Education* 119: 5–15.

Tyack, D. B. (1974). *The one best system: A history of American urban education.* Cambridge, MA: Harvard University Press.

Vermette, P., L. Harper, and S. DiMillo. (2004). Cooperative and collaborative learning with 4–8 year olds: How does research support teachers' practice? *Journal of Instructional Psychology* 3 (2): 130–34.

Walther-Thomas, C., L. Korinek, and V. McLaughlin. (1999). Collaboration to support students' success. *Focus on Exceptional Children* 32 (3): 1–8.

Weber, E. (1984). *Ideas influencing early childhood education.* New York: Teachers College Press.

Wenger, E. (1998). *Communities of practice: Learning, meaning and identity.* Cambridge, UK: Cambridge University Press.

Wenger, E. (2000a). Communities of practice and learning systems. *Organization* 7 (2): 225–46.

Wenger, E. (2000b). Communities of practice: Stewarding knowledge. In *Knowledge horizons: The present and the promise of knowledge management*, ed. C. Despres and D. Chauvel. Boston: Butterworth-Heinemann.

Wurm, J. P. (2005). *Working in the Reggio way: A beginner's guide for American teachers.* St. Paul: Redleaf.

Yinger, R. (1990). The conversation of practice. In *Encouraging reflective practice in education*, ed. R. T. Clift, W. R. Houston, and M. C. Pugach, 73–96. New York: Teachers College Press.

Appendix

Fetherston, B., and R. Kelly. (2007). Conflict resolution and transformative pedagogy: A grounded theory research project on learning in higher education. *Journal of Transformative Education* 5 (3): 262–85.

Mezirow, J. (1975). *Education for perspective transformation: Women's reentry programs in community colleges.* New York: Center for Adult Education Teachers College, Columbia University.

Mezirow, J. (1978). Perspective transformation. *Adult Education* 28 (2): 100–110.

Mezirow, J. (1981). A critical theory of adult learning and education. *Adult Education* 32 (1): 3–23.

Mezirow, J. (1995). Transformation theory of adult learning. In *In defense of the lifeworld*, ed. M. R. Welton, 39–70. New York: State University of New York Press.

Mezirow, J. (1997). Transformative learning: Theory to practice. In *Transformative learning in action: Insights from practice*, ed. P. Cranton, 5–12. San Francisco: Jossey-Bass.

Mezirow, J. (2000). *Learning as transformation: Critical perspectives on a theory in progress.* San Francisco: Jossey-Bass.